TRANSIT COOPERATIVE RESEARCH PROGRAM

Report 41

New Designs and Operating Experiences with Low-Floor Buses

ROLLAND D. KING
Columbus, OH

Subject Areas

Public Transit

Research Sponsored by the Federal Transit Administration in Cooperation with the Transit Development Corporation

TRANSPORTATION RESEARCH BOARD
NATIONAL RESEARCH COUNCIL

NATIONAL ACADEMY PRESS
Washington, D.C. 1998

TRANSIT COOPERATIVE RESEARCH PROGRAM

The nation's growth and the need to meet mobility, environmental, and energy objectives place demands on public transit systems. Current systems, some of which are old and in need of upgrading, must expand service area, increase service frequency, and improve efficiency to serve these demands. Research is necessary to solve operating problems, to adapt appropriate new technologies from other industries, and to introduce innovations into the transit industry. The Transit Cooperative Research Program (TCRP) serves as one of the principal means by which the transit industry can develop innovative near-term solutions to meet demands placed on it.

The need for TCRP was originally identified in *TRB Special Report 213—Research for Public Transit: New Directions*, published in 1987 and based on a study sponsored by the Urban Mass Transportation Administration—now the Federal Transit Administration (FTA). A report by the American Public Transit Association (APTA), *Transportation 2000*, also recognized the need for local, problem-solving research. TCRP, modeled after the longstanding and successful National Cooperative Highway Research Program, undertakes research and other technical activities in response to the needs of transit service providers. The scope of TCRP includes a variety of transit research fields including planning, service configuration, equipment, facilities, operations, human resources, maintenance, policy, and administrative practices.

TCRP was established under FTA sponsorship in July 1992. Proposed by the U.S. Department of Transportation, TCRP was authorized as part of the Intermodal Surface Transportation Efficiency Act of 1991 (ISTEA). On May 13, 1992, a memorandum agreement outlining TCRP operating procedures was executed by the three cooperating organizations: FTA; the National Academy of Sciences, acting through the **Transportation Research Board (TRB)**; and the Transit Development Corporation, Inc. (TDC), a nonprofit educational and research organization established by APTA. TDC is responsible for forming the independent governing board, designated as the TCRP Oversight and Project Selection (TOPS) Committee.

Research problem statements for TCRP are solicited periodically but may be submitted to TRB by anyone at any time It is the responsibility of the TOPS Committee to formulate the research program by identifying the highest priority projects. As part of the evaluation, the TOPS Committee defines funding levels and expected products.

Once selected, each project is assigned to an expert panel, appointed by the Transportation Research Board. The panels prepare project statements (requests for proposals), select contractors, and provide technical guidance and counsel throughout the life of the project. The process for developing research problem statements and selecting research agencies has been used by TRB in managing cooperative research programs since 1962. As in other TRB activities, TCRP project panels serve voluntarily without compensation.

Because research cannot have the desired impact if products fail to reach the intended audience, special emphasis is placed on disseminating TCRP results to the intended end users of the research: transit agencies, service providers, and suppliers. TRB provides a series of research reports, syntheses of transit practice, and other supporting material developed by TCRP research. APTA will arrange for workshops, training aids, field visits, and other activities to ensure that results are implemented by urban and rural transit industry practitioners.

The TCRP provides a forum where transit agencies can cooperatively address common operational problems. The TCRP results support and complement other ongoing transit research and training programs.

TCRP REPORT 41

Project C-10C FY'96
ISSN 1073-4872
ISBN 0-309-06308-6
Library of Congress Catalog Card No. 98-61202

© 1998 Transportation Research Board

Price $28.00

NOTICE

The project that is the subject of this report was a part of the Transit Cooperative Research Program conducted by the Transportation Research Board with the approval of the Governing Board of the National Research Council. Such approval reflects the Governing Board's judgment that the project concerned is appropriate with respect to both the purposes and resources of the National Research Council.

The members of the technical advisory panel selected to monitor this project and to review this report were chosen for recognized scholarly competence and with due consideration for the balance of disciplines appropriate to the project. The opinions and conclusions expressed or implied are those of the research agency that performed the research, and while they have been accepted as appropriate by the technical panel, they are not necessarily those of the Transportation Research Board, the National Research Council, the Transit Development Corporation, or the Federal Transit Administration of the U.S. Department of Transportation.

Each report is reviewed and accepted for publication by the technical panel according to procedures established and monitored by the Transportation Research Board Executive Committee and the Governing Board of the National Research Council.

To save time and money in disseminating the research findings, the report is essentially the original text as submitted by the research agency. This report has not been edited by TRB.

Special Notice

The Transportation Research Board, the National Research Council, the Transit Development Corporation, and the Federal Transit Administration (sponsor of the Transit Cooperative Research Program) do not endorse products or manufacturers. Trade or manufacturers' names appear herein solely because they are considered essential to the clarity and completeness of the project reporting.

Published reports of the

TRANSIT COOPERATIVE RESEARCH PROGRAM

are available from:

Transportation Research Board
National Research Council
2101 Constitution Avenue, N.W.
Washington, D.C. 20418

and can be ordered through the Internet at
http://www.nas.edu/trb/index.html

Printed in the United States of America

FOREWORD

By Staff
Transportation Research
Board

This report will be of interest to transit managers, policymakers, operations and maintenance professionals, bus procurement specialists, bus manufacturers and suppliers, and others interested in operating experience to date with low-floor transit buses. The report provides information on the current market for low-floor buses and provides a summary of operating experiences on the basis of discussions with transit agencies and low-floor bus manufacturers. The report includes information on customer satisfaction and acceptance, bus capacity and ridership impacts, bus operating experiences, impacts on maintenance and facilities, safety experiences, and operator and mechanic acceptance and satisfaction. Also included is a discussion of the current market and market trends for low-floor buses, an update of the status of low-floor bus technology and technological developments, and a summary of key specifications for low-floor buses available to the North American transit market. This report will be particularly useful for transit agencies considering the deployment of low-floor transit buses.

TCRP Synthesis 2, "Low-Floor Transit Buses," described the technology and issues associated with low-floor transit buses as of January 1994. However, much has taken place in the marketplace since that time. Low-floor bus technology has been evolving rapidly, new designs have been introduced, and low-floor buses have generally been in revenue service over a longer period of time, logging well over 100 million miles of service to date. Accordingly, transit managers seek objective information concerning the latest operating experiences of low-floor buses, as well as the most recent status of the low-floor bus market to assist them with their purchasing decisions.

Under TCRP Project C-10C, research was undertaken by Rolland D. King to gather and synthesize information available on the low-floor bus marketplace, and to report on the experiences of transit agencies currently operating low-floor buses.

To achieve the project objectives, the researcher made site visits to 10 transit agencies operating low-floor buses. Site visits were made to the Ann Arbor Transportation Authority, Calgary Transit, Champaign-Urbana Mass Transit District, Capital District Transportation Authority (Albany, NY), Chicago Transit Authority, Metropolitan Atlanta Rapid Transit Authority, Milwaukee County Transit System, Phoenix Transit System, Société de Transport de la Communauté Urbaine de Montréal, and Société de Transport de la Rive-Sud de Montréal. During the site visits, information on experience with low-floor buses was obtained through interviews with management, staff, and passengers. Information from several additional transit agencies was also obtained by telephone. In a number of cases, internal reports on low-floor bus operating experiences were provided.

A survey of the six bus manufactures offering heavy-duty, standard-sized, low-floor buses to the North American transit market was also conducted to obtain low-floor bus market and trend information. Bus specification information was also collected, including clearances, entrance heights, wheelbase, seating capacity, type of floor (e.g., step, slope, flat), sizes of buses offered, empty vehicle weight, and GVWR. Bus manufacturers surveyed included Gillig, Neoplan USA, New Flyer Industries, North American Bus Industries, Nova Bus, and Orion Bus Industries.

Finally, a review of the technical literature from the United States, Canada, and Europe concerning low-floor bus experiences, technological developments, and practices was conducted.

CONTENTS

i   **Executive Summary**

1   **1.0 Introduction**
       1.1 Background, 1
       1.2 Approach, 2

4   **2.0 Operating Experiences with Low-Floor Buses**
       2.1 Customer Satisfaction and Acceptance, 4
       2.2 Customer Comfort and Environment Issues, 13
       2.3 Capacity and Ridership Impacts, 20
       2.4 Impacts on Ridership, 31
       2.5 Vehicle Operating Experiences, 33
       2.6 Impacts on Maintenance and Facilities, 34
       2.7 Safety Experiences, 38
       2.8 Operator and Mechanic Acceptance and Satisfaction, 41

44   **3.0 Market Status and Trends**

47   **4.0 Technology Status and Developments**
       4.1 Status of Bus Manufacturers, 47
       4.2 Developments in Technology, 47

56   **5.0 Conclusions and Recommendations**
       5.1 Conclusions, 56
       5.2 Recommendations, 63

65   **References**

68   **Acronyms and Abbreviations**

A-1   **APPENDIX A**   **Technical Description of Low-Floor Fleets**

B-1   **APPENDIX B**   **Discussions of Factors Impacting Capacity**

C-1   **APPENDIX C**   **Interview Guide and Survey Form**

D-1   **APPENDIX D**   **Listing of Participants**

COOPERATIVE RESEARCH PROGRAMS STAFF

ROBERT J. REILLY, *Director, Cooperative Research Programs*
STEPHEN J. ANDRLE, *Manager, Transit Cooperative Research Program*
CHRISTOPHER W. JENKS, *Senior Program Officer*
EILEEN P. DELANEY, *Managing Editor*
HILARY FREER, *Assistant Editor*

PROJECT PANEL C-10

WINFORD L. TERRENTINE, *Chagrin Falls, OH* (Chair)
SAMY E. G. ELIAS, *University of Nebraska–Lincoln*
ROBERT L. GRAHAM, *Northrop Grumman Corporation, El Segundo, CA*
BRENDON HEMILY, *Canadian Urban Transit Association, Toronto*
DANA LOWELL, *MTA New York City Transit*
JAMES McDOWELL, *Nova Bus, Inc., Roswell, NM*
JAMES L. O'SULLIVAN, *Fleet Maintenance Consultants, Houston, TX*
RONALD J. SHIPLEY, *Pierce Transit, Tacoma, WA*
JERRY TROTTER, *APTA*
FRANK W. VENEZIA, *Lea & Elliott, Downers Grove, IL*
SHANG QUEN HSIUNG, *FTA Liaison Representative*
WILLIAM MENCZER, *FTA Liaison Representative*
PETER SHAW, *TRB Liaison Representative*

AUTHOR ACKNOWLEDGMENTS

Rolland King, Columbus, Ohio, was responsible for the collection of data and preparation of the report. KyLynn Slayton provided valuable assistance in the preparation of the report.

The author acknowledges with thanks the time and valuable assistance of many people at transit agencies and bus manufacturers who provided information for this report. Valuable assistance was provided by panel members in the preparation of this report. TCRP Program Officer Christopher Jenks deserves many thanks for his help and support throughout this project.

EXECUTIVE SUMMARY

Since their deployment in 1991, low-floor buses have increasingly become the choice of transit agencies in both the United States and Canada. At the close of 1997, there were over 2,800 low-floor buses in operation, and another 2,660 on order in North America. Since their introduction in 1991, low-floor buses in North America have logged well over 100-million miles in revenue service.

The most frequent reason given by transit agencies for choosing a low-floor bus was to provide a more user-friendly, easier access for all customers -- adults, children, people with disabilities, seniors, people carrying infants or with strollers, and people with packages. Other reasons include: to meet the Americans with Disabilities Act (ADA) accessibility requirements using ramps rather than lifts, and to provide transit service for the growing population of elderly customers with fixed-route service rather than special transportation service.

In the United States, the enactment of the ADA has been a major force in the growing interest in low-floor buses. In Canada, several provinces have encouraged the purchase of low-floor buses in the form of policy directives and funding incentives.

The objectives of this project were to collect and synthesize information available on the operating experiences of transit agencies that currently operate low-floor buses, including user acceptance, safety considerations, service impacts, operator acceptance, ridership impacts, and maintenance impacts. In addition, information on the trends and market outlook for low-floor buses was to be provided. The focus of the project was on the experiences with the standard-size, heavy-duty, low-floor buses.

The approach used to gather the desired information was a combination of: interviews of transit agencies at their facilities, telephone interviews with other transit agencies, survey of the bus manufacturers, and a review of the technical literature. Ten agencies were selected for site visits, and six bus manufacturers were surveyed.

The overall experience with low-floor buses in the United States and Canada has been positive, according to the interviews. Many of the early problems experienced by the agencies interviewed appear to be new bus problems rather than problems intrinsically related to a low-floor bus design. The significant findings from the interviews with transit agencies operating low-floor buses and discussions with bus manufacturers are provided below.

Customer Issues

All customers liked the ease of boarding and alighting in the low-floor bus. Seniors and people with disabilities expressed an even stronger preference. In general, ramps were preferred to lifts.

Customers also liked the improved visibility provided by the larger windows, the feeling of a spacious environment with the higher ceilings, and places to put packages.

Customers had complaints and concerns. The most frequent complaint was the lack of seats. Some complained about crowding, noise and vibration, fogged windows, cold feet, and "jerky" ride. Some customers expressed concern about the steps in the aisle. Only one agency had received many strong complaints about crowding on their low-floor buses from their customers.

Capacity Issues

All of the current low-floor buses have less seats than comparable high-floor buses, 31 to 40 for low-floor buses compared to 43 to 45 for high-floor buses. If an agency's loading standard is to provide a seat for all expected customers, then the loss in capacity would be proportional to the loss of seats.

Eight of the transit agencies interviewed had not made changes in their schedules or the number of buses used with the introduction of low-floor buses to their fleets. Two agencies thought that the lower capacity of their low-floor buses would require more buses to be added to routes. One agency, in an effort to relieve the crowding and congestion in their low-floor buses, was evaluating a new interior design for their buses, and believed that the new interior design would provide them with a total capacity for their low-floor buses equal to their current high-floor buses.

Boarding times for ambulatory passengers were reported to be faster with low-floor buses, from 0.2 to 0.7 of a second. The average boarding time of wheelchair passengers was faster with the ramp than with a lift, 27.4 seconds versus 46.4 seconds. While these shorter boarding/ alighting times had not resulted in increases in schedule speed at any of the transit agencies interviewed, some felt that the faster ramp operations made it easier to maintain schedule, particularly when multiple wheelchair boardings occurred during a run.

Vehicle Operating and Maintenance Experiences

A summary of significant operating and maintenance experiences reported by the agencies is provided below:

- All were generally satisfied with the road clearance capabilities of the low-floor buses. Occasional groundings were reported for some high railroad crossings and on steep ramps.
- Operators reported that the low-floor buses were quicker (higher acceleration) and had good handling characteristics.
- The ramp was popular with everyone. Road calls because of ramp failures were reported as rare to none. Maintenance on a ramp is much less than on a lift.
- All transit agencies were using a low profile, radial tire on their low-floor buses. All reported from 20 to 30 percent less life with their low profile tires. Also, some agencies reported frequent wheel damage from hitting the curb during turns.
- Brakes were reported as a problem at most agencies. The major problems were: brake effort balance between front and rear brakes, timing of brake application, and the short life of brake linings. A retrofit program has corrected the first two problems. The life of brake

linings is improving. The problems with the brakes appear to have resulted because the bus was a new bus design rather than a low-floor design.

- Changes in the maintenance facilities have been minimal. No changes to pits had been made. Some agencies had fabricated fixtures to adapt their existing hoist for the low-floor buses. Some used ladders and others used movable platforms to work on roof mounted components. Minor adjustments to bus wash brush height were made by some agencies to accommodate the lower side skirts on low-floor buses. As with any new bus, some additional tooling and maintenance equipment was required.
- Overall, the operators liked their low-floor buses. Operators liked the ease of customer boarding, the ease of using the ramp, the quickness and handling of the bus, the improved visibility, and the eye level contact with customers.
- Mechanics were generally satisfied with the low-floor buses. Some preferred to work on the low-floor buses because everything was cleaner and accessible, while others expressed some concerns about working from ladders and elevated platforms.

Safety Experiences

All transit agencies were satisfied with their safety experiences with their low-floor buses. However, none had conducted an investigation to support their perceptions. At this early stage of deployment, a statistically valid comparison of passenger safety for low-floor buses versus high-floor buses could not be made from the available data. A summary of reported experiences are given below.

- Four agencies reported that the number of passenger accidents per low-floor bus was higher than the passenger accidents per bus for their high-floor fleet. <u>All</u> agencies cautioned against making a simple comparison of the data because the exposure of the low-floor buses (more passengers and more miles per bus) was higher than for their high-floor buses.
- Some agencies felt that the higher frequency of slips and falls of passengers occurring in front of the low-floor buses could be related to the lack of an adequate number of handholds from the farebox to the first row of seats.
- All agencies reported that no safety incidents had occurred because of the steps in the aisle.

With six suppliers, the growth in sales of low-floor buses in the last two years has grown rapidly. In 1997, there were 1,185 low-floor buses delivered to transit agencies in North America. Three of the manufacturers estimated that their sales in

2000 would be 50 to 90 percent low-floor models.

Several R&D programs that hold promise to provide improvements in low-floor bus technology in the future are suggested. Research needs that were identified are: the development of level boarding with low-floor buses, development of improved handholds for the front of the bus, and an investigation into methods to reduce dwell times.

1.0 INTRODUCTION

1.1 Background

Transit systems in North America began to use low-floor transit buses in December 1991. Over 2,800 standard and large-size, low-floor buses were in revenue service by the end of 1997, and another 2,660 were on order. Since their introduction in 1991, low-floor buses in North America have logged well over 100-million miles of revenue service.

The most frequent reason given by transit agencies for choosing a low-floor bus was to provide a more user-friendly, easier access for all customers -- adults, children, people with disabilities, seniors, people carrying infants or with strollers, and people with packages. The reasons for choosing low-floor buses varied from agency to agency, but the three most frequent cited were:

- To provide an easier more user-friendly access for all passengers,
- To meet the Americans with Disabilities Act (ADA) accessibility requirements using ramp technology, and avoiding the high maintenance cost and unreliability of lifts, and
- To provide transit service for the growing population of elderly customers with fixed-route service rather than special transportation service.

As interest in the purchase of these new buses grew, more transit managers began seeking objective information on topics such as: fewer seats, customer acceptance and satisfaction, ridership impacts, maintenance costs, vehicle handling and road clearances, and safety. A project under the Transit Cooperative Research Program (TCRP) was established to update and expand on the information provided in an earlier TCRP synthesis report on low-floor buses (Reference 1). The synthesis report focused on low-floor bus technology since the deployment of low-floor buses in North America had just begun and very limited operating experience data were available at that time. In June 1997, a contract was issued to gather and synthesize information available on the operating experiences of transit agencies that currently operate low-floor buses, including user acceptance, safety considerations, service impacts, operator acceptance, ridership impacts, and maintenance impacts. In addition, information on the transit agencies currently operating low-floor buses, as well as information on the trends and market outlook for low-floor buses was to be provided. The results of that project are contained in this report.

What makes a bus a low-floor bus? A widely accepted definition for a low-floor bus that was first proposed to the International Union of Public Transportation (UITP) in 1991 (Reference 2), and is applicable today is as follows:

> "The low-floor bus is a bus which, between doors 1 and 2, has a vehicle floor sufficiently low and level enough to remove the need for steps in the aisle both between these doors, and in the vicinity of the doors."

The basic issue is how to provide a low, flat floor at entrances and over the axle areas.

An entrance level of 380 mm (15 inches) or less is required to provide access to the bus floor without steps at the entrance door. Either a deep drop beam or an independent axle approach is used for the front axle to provide a low level floor access to the passenger area. In North America, two approaches are also used to clear the rear axle and other drive train components. One approach has been to use steps from the low front floor area to an elevated floor area in the rear of the bus. The other approach is to use a ramp in the floor to clear a drop center rear axle. More information on the various low-floor bus technologies can be found in References 1, 2, and 3.

1.2   Approach

The approach used to gather the desired information was a combination of: interviews of transit agencies at their facilities, telephone interviews with other transit agencies, surveys of the bus manufacturers, and review of the technical literature. The transit agencies identified for site visits were diversified as to operating environments, such as: climates, passenger loads, and fleet size, and low-floor bus technologies. Site visits were made to: Ann Arbor Transportation Authority, Calgary Transit, Champaign-Urbana Mass Transit District, Capital District Transportation Authority, Chicago Transit Authority, Metropolitan Atlanta Rapid Transit Authority, Milwaukee County Transit System, Phoenix Transit System, Société de Transport de la Communauté Urbaine de Montréal, and Société de Transport de la Rive-Sud de Montréal.

During the site visits, information was obtained through interviews with management, staff, and passengers. A copy of the interview guide used during the site visits is in Appendix C. Several of these agencies also provided internal reports on their operating experiences. In addition, telephone interviews were held with several other transit agencies that were identified during the course of the project as having significant information.

A survey was sent to the six bus manufacturers that are offering heavy-duty, standard-size, low-floor buses to the North American transit market. The survey requested both technical and marketing information. A copy of the bus manufacturers' survey is in Appendix C. The final source of information for this study was the literature from the U.S., Canada, and Europe on low-floor bus experiences, technology developments, and practices.

This report is divided into five major sections, starting with this brief introduction. The second section provides detailed discussions of the operating experiences reported by the transit agencies interviewed. The third section describes the status and trends of the low-floor bus market. The fourth section discusses the developments in low-floor bus technologies and some of the emerging practices in Europe. Conclusions and recommendations for future research are provided in the last section. The Appendices contain technical information of the low-floor fleets at the transit agencies interviewed, copies of the interview guide and survey forms, a discussion of vehicle and operational factors that impact capacity, and a listing of agencies and manufacturers that provided information for this report.

Since low-floor bus developments and operating experiences are rapidly changing, it is likely that some of the details of what transit agencies are experiencing and bus manufacturers are doing is changing. However, it is hoped that this report will convey some useful information about the "lessons learned," an understanding of what technologies are available, and be useful to those considering the purchase of low-floor buses.

2.0 OPERATING EXPERIENCES WITH LOW-FLOOR BUSES

The operating experiences with low-floor buses reported in this report were largely obtained from interviews of twelve transit agencies. Some additional operating experiences that were found in the open literature are also included. Operating experiences were obtained from low-floor fleets of different: sizes, passenger loadings, geographic locations, climate conditions, and low-floor bus technologies. Selected operational statistics for the twelve agencies that participated in the study are given in Table 2.1. Information on the twelve low-floor bus fleets is given in Table 2.2. A more complete technical description of the fleets can be found in Appendix A.

Information was gathered on customer acceptance and satisfaction, capacity and ridership impacts, experiences with the vehicle in revenue service, maintenance issues, safety issues, and operator and mechanic acceptance. The interview findings for each of these topics are discussed in the following paragraphs.

2.1 Customer Satisfaction and Acceptance

All of the transit agencies interviewed reported that their customers liked the ease of boarding and alighting of the low-floor buses. This was the case for all customers, and was particularly true for seniors and customers with disabilities. This perception is supported by all of the customer satisfaction surveys that were conducted by the agencies. Overall, customer satisfaction and acceptance of the low-floor buses has been positive. All agencies have received the occasional customer complaint on issues such as: lack of seats, cold feet, noise and vibration, fogged windows (can't see out), and jerky ride. The Société de Transport de la Communauté Urbaine de Montréal (STCUM) was the only system in this study that experienced a high level of customer complaints with the low-floor buses. The reasons for customer dissatisfaction at STCUM are complex, and appear to be related to a combination of interior design factors that were exacerbated by extremely high loading factors. These issues are discussed in a later section. It is interesting to note that the Société de Transport de la Rive-Sud de Montréal (STRSM) has the same low-floor bus in revenue service, and they reported that their customers liked the bus.

2.1.1 Customer Satisfaction Surveys

Several transit agencies have conducted satisfaction and acceptance surveys of their customers and operators shortly after the introduction of low-floor buses in their fleets (References 4, 5, 6, 7, 8, 9, 10, and 11). In general, the acceptance of the low-floor buses was found to be positive. However, there were concerns reported in some of the surveys. The significant findings of these surveys are discussed in the following paragraphs.

Table 2.1 Statistics of Bus Operations of Systems Providing Information[a]

TRANSIT AGENCY	ANNUAL UNLINKED TRIPS (total bus fleet)	UNLINKED PASSENGER TRIPS[b]		VEHICLE UTILIZATION[c] in miles/vehicle	AVERAGE SPEED[d] in mph	SIZE OF ACTIVE BUS FLEET
		per VEH-HR	per VEH-MILE			
Ann Arbor Transportation Authority	3,831,861	23.79	1.69	36,651	14.11	62
BC Transit - Victoria Regional Transit System	20,076,344	38.5	2.89	36,601	13.3	190
Calgary Transit	52,224,700	43.47	2.86	32,184	15.2	568
Champaign-Urbana Mass Transit District	8,806,274	49.32	3.91	30,000	12.6	75
Capital District Transportation Authority	11,330,369	25.63	2.19	23,082	11.70	224
Chicago Transit Authority	302,115,116	45.60	4.50	33,961	10.12	1,975
Metropolitan Atlanta Rapid Transit Authority	72,295,000	35.38	2.76	38,204	12.8	685
Milwaukee County Transit System	59,988,056	42.18	3.50	32,639	12.04	525
Phoenix Transit System	28,705,464	46.76	3.02	27,565	15.49	345
Sault Ste. Marie Transit	1,500,000	20.75	1.61	38,750	12.86	24
Société Transport de la Communauté Urbaine de Montréal (STCUM)	248,660,000	54.58	5.49	29,220	9.94	1,550
Société de Transport de la Rive-Sud de Montréal (STRSM)	26,821,320	38.40	2.64	30,985	14.5	330

[a] 1996 data from the National Transit Database and the Canadian Urban Transit Association Operating Statistics.
[b] Unlinked Trips/Revenue Vehicle-Hours and Unlinked Trip/Revenue Vehicle-Miles.
[c] Revenue Vehicle Miles/Vehicles in Active Fleet.
[d] Revenue Vehicle Miles/Revenue Vehicle Hours.

Table 2.2 Low-Floor Fleets Included in Study

TRANSIT AGENCY	FLEET NO.	SIZE (ft.)	MANUFACTURER & MODEL	
Ann Arbor Transportation Authority	22 15	40 35	New Flyer Industries	D40LF D35LF
BC Transit - Victoria Regional Transit System	36 44	40 40	New Flyer Industries	D40LF
Calgary Transit	50 84	40 40	New Flyer Industries	D40LF
Champaign-Urbana Mass Transit District	41	40	New Flyer Industries	D40LF
Capital District Transportation Authority	21	40	Orion Bus Industries	ORION VI
Chicago Transit Authority	65 1	40 40	New Flyer Industries	D40LF H40LF
Metropolitan Atlanta Rapid Transit Authority	118 51	40 40	New Flyer Industries	C40LF D40LF
Milwaukee County Transit System	146	40	New Flyer Industries	D40LF
Phoenix Transit System	93	40	New Flyer Industries	D40LF
Sault Ste. Marie Transit	4	40	Orion Bus Industries	ORION VI
Société Transport de la Communauté Urbaine de Montréal (STCUM)	270	40	Nova Bus	LFS
Société de Transport de la Rive-Sud de Montréal (STRSM)	28	40	Nova Bus	LFS

2.1.1.1 Ann Arbor Transportation Authority. An on-board survey (Reference 4) conducted in July 1994 at the Ann Arbor Transportation Authority (AATA), found that most customers, including those who have some difficulty with steps, found low-floor buses easier to use. As shown in Table 2.3, most customers (both those with no difficulty and those with difficulty) found the low-floor bus easier to get on and off. For other issues: availability of seats, ease of getting to a seat, seat comfort, smoothness of ride, and feeling of personal security, less than 50 percent of the customers had a preference for low-floor buses. However, for none of the survey

Table 2.3 Percent of Riders Preferring Low-Floor Buses at AATA

	No Difficulty with Steps (n=256)	Some Difficulty with Steps (n=56)
Ease of getting on the bus	82%	89%
Ease of getting to a seat	41%	48%
Ease of leaving the bus	72%	75%
Availability of seats	34%	44%
Seated comfort	39%	38%
Feeling of roominess	63%	59%
Smoothness of the ride	47%	46%
Feeling of personal security	25%	29%
Ability to see out	60%	63%

Source: Reference 4

measurements did more than 15 percent of the customers prefer high-floor buses, and the balance stated that they had no preference.

2.1.1.2 Calgary Transit. In September 1993, Calgary Transit (CT) began operating 50 New Flyer Industries D40L low-floor buses. On a Thursday early in December of that year, a survey was distributed to riders of low-floor buses on six routes. The purpose of the survey was to receive and evaluate some low-floor features and performance of the buses. A total of 400 surveys were distributed and 351 (88%) were returned (Reference 5).

Customers were asked to rate several features of the low-floor buses as being either good, fair, or poor. The major findings of the survey are shown in Table 4.2. As can be seen in Table 2.4, most customers liked the ease of boarding. The customer concerns about handrails related to the location and number at the front of the bus. Most customers thought there should be more handrails or straps, and that they should be lowered or easier to reach. This feature resulted in the second highest number of critical comments. A number of customers said that the rear doors were either too hard to open or that the doors closed too quickly. While the majority of customers rated the general ride quality as good, the reviews were mixed in that about one-third thought the ride was rough. Some customers did not like the elevated rear

Table 2.4 Customer Responses to Calgary Transit Survey of Low-Floor Buses

Feature	Good	Fair	Poor	No Answer
Front Entrance	92%	5%	2%	1%
Location of Hand Rails	56%	30%	13%	1%
Rear Exit	77%	14%	6%	3%
General Ride Comfort	69%	21%	8%	2%
Side Windows	85%	10%	3%	2%
Elevated Area at Rear	59%	23%	13%	6%
Heating	72%	21%	5%	2%
Number of Seats	38%	30%	30%	1%
Overall Bus Rating	71%	22%	5%	2%

Source: Reference 5

seating area; either they did not like having to climb steps, they felt the steps were a bottleneck, or they perceived that the area was reserved for younger passengers. The need for better heat distribution, particularly onto the side windows, was mentioned by some customers. The feature that received the most criticism was seating capacity. Over 25 percent of the respondents said that the low-floor buses did not have enough seats. There also were comments that the bus did not have sufficient capacity for rush hour service.

2.1.1.3 Chicago Transit Authority.
In July 1992, a low-floor bus (New Flyer, D40L) was made available to the Chicago Transit Authority (CTA) for in-service testing. The bus was operated in revenue service on two routes (79 and 22) and was made available for inspection displays at several locations. Customer response surveys were conducted of passengers riding along the routes and at the on-display locations. Surveys were also conducted of passengers along the same routes riding the CTA's current high-floor buses (Flxible and TMC lift equipped buses that were purchased in 1990-91). There were 832 survey responses of the low-floor bus, 644 survey responses of the TMC buses, and 613 survey responses of the Flxible buses (Reference 6).

There were 99 respondents that used some type of mobility aid (i.e., cane, walker, crutches, or wheelchair). There were 194 respondents who used or "tried-out" the ramp or used a lift to get on the bus. The respondents who used a mobility aid were asked to rate the ease of using a ramp or lift. In response to the questions, "If you used the ramp (lift), please indicate how easy it was," the responses shown in Table 2.5 were given. Approximately 96 percent found the ramp easy to very easy to use and only about one percent said that it was hard or very hard to use. In comparison, 70 percent said that the lift was easy to very easy to use and approximately 13 percent reported lift use as hard to very hard.

The survey contained a number of statements relating to attributes of a bus. The respondents were asked their degree of agreement or disagreement with the statements. Table 2.6 provides the customer responses to statements relating to quality of service for low-floor and high-floor buses. It can be seen from the responses in Table 2.6 that the low-floor bus was preferred over the high-floor buses for all of these statements of service quality.

2.1.1.4 Metropolitan Atlanta Rapid Transit Authority. In the Fall of 1994, the Metropolitan Atlanta Rapid Transit Authority (MARTA) purchased 51 New Flyer D40L low-floor buses. In February 1995, MARTA conducted a customer survey to evaluate their satisfaction with the new low-floor buses. The survey was conducted on-board by MARTA staff. To assure a random sample, every fifth customer was asked to respond to several survey statements. A total of 712 surveys were completed. Twenty-eight identified themselves as physically disabled, and three were using wheelchairs. Over three-fourths (78 percent) were daily riders. The trip purpose was divided as: over one-half (57 percent) was commute to work, about 15 percent were students, and the remainder were on personal business journeys. About one-third (31 percent) of the respondents had ridden low-floor buses more than 15 times, and about five percent were first time riders of the low-floor bus (Reference 7).

Table 2.5 CTA Survey Findings on Ease of Using Ramp/Lift to Board Bus

Access	Number of Respondents	Very Easy	Easy	Neutral	Hard	Very Hard
Ramp	134	109 (81.3)(*)	19 (14.2)	4 (3.0)	1 (0.7)	1 (0.7)
Lift	60	17 (28.3)	25 (41.7)	10 (16.7)	6 (10.0)	2 (3.3)

Source: Reference 6

(*) Numbers in parentheses are in percent of total responses.

Table 2.6 Customer Responses to CTA Survey Statements Related to Quality of Service

Statement	Bus(*)	Strongly Agree	Agree Somewhat	Neutral	Disagree Somewhat	Strongly Disagree	Total No. of Responses
This bus was easy to board.	New Flyer	72.6%	12.9%	6.4%	1.8%	6.2%	760
	Flxible	7.7%	6.0%	11.2%	20.3%	54.7%	581
	TMC	52.4%	20.7%	12.9%	4.6%	9.5%	613
It was easy to get to the seats.	New Flyer	55.5%	19.8%	11.3%	6.1%	7.2%	732
	Flxible	53.0%	19.9%	11.9%	8.0%	7.1%	562
	TMC	45.1%	23.9%	13.5%	8.2%	9.3%	599
The bus ride is smooth.	New Flyer	45.9%	26.4%	16.0%	5.0%	6.7%	643
	Flxible	21.9%	30.2%	21.5%	15.8%	10.6%	539
	TMC	17.8%	24.8%	25.0%	18.6%	13.8%	580
Overall, this is a comfortable bus.	New Flyer	50.0%	25.6%	12.7%	4.8%	6.9%	714
	Flxible	33.0%	31.8%	20.9%	8.1%	6.1%	554
	TMC	8.9%	9.4%	22.9%	32.2%	26.5%	593
It is easy to get to the back seating area.	New Flyer	42.2%	25.9%	15.4%	7.8%	8.7%	618

(*) The New Flyer bus was a low-floor bus, all others were high-floor buses.

Source: Reference 6

Customers were asked their preferences on several attributes of the low-floor bus versus the conventional MARTA high-floor buses. The major findings were:

- A large majority of the customers found the low-floor buses easier to board and alight (84 percent and 81 percent, respectively), and only about 2 percent said that boarding and alighting was more difficult.
- Slightly over one-half of the customers found it easier to get to a seat on the low-floor bus (55 percent), while 10 percent found it more difficult.
- Less than one-half of the customers said that it was easier to get a seat (44 percent), and

about one-fifth (20 percent) said that it was more difficult.
- Most customers (92 percent) rated the low-floor buses as having good or excellent visibility while only two-thirds of the customers rated the conventional MARTA buses as having good or excellent visibility.
- Most customers (91 percent) gave the low-floor buses a good or excellent overall rating while only 60 percent gave the conventional MARTA buses a good or excellent rating.
- Most customers (76 percent) said that low-floor buses provided good or excellent package handling. While slightly less than one-half (48 percent) rated the conventional MARTA buses as providing good or excellent package handling aspects. Over one-fourth of the respondents had at least one package at the time of the survey.
- A large majority (94 percent) rated the low-floor buses good or excellent in regards to being safe to board while just over one-half (56 percent) gave the same rating to the conventional MARTA buses.

2.1.1.5 Metropolitan Transit Authority of Harris County. In July 1997, the Metropolitan Transit Authority of Harris County (MTA) conducted a customer satisfaction survey of their new low-floor buses (Reference 8). Surveys were distributed to riders on-board the low-floor buses on one route. Of the 450 surveys given out, 144 completed surveys were returned for a response rate of 32 percent. A summary of the major findings follows.

- Overall satisfaction with the low-floor bus was 72 percent, and only 7 percent of the respondents were not satisfied.
- About one-half (47 percent) of the respondents felt that the low-floor buses were better compared to other metro buses, while 19 percent thought that the conventional metro buses were better.
- Over three-fourths (76 percent) of the respondents said that the overall quality of ride was better on the low-floor buses, and 10 percent were dissatisfied.
- Most (88 percent) of the survey respondents were satisfied with the ease of boarding the low-floor buses.
- Over three-fourths (76 percent) of the respondents were satisfied with the ease of exiting the rear door of the low-floor buses.
- Most (82 percent) of the survey respondents were satisfied with the steps up to the back seats.
- Over three-fourths (78 percent) of the survey respondents were satisfied with width of the aisle.
- Most (80 percent) of the respondents were satisfied with the visibility from inside the low-floor buses.
- About three-fourths (72 percent) were satisfied with the interior noise level of the low-floor buses.

- About three-fourths (71 percent) of the survey respondents were satisfied with the number of seats.
- The respondents strongly preferred forward-facing seats. They were willing to trade almost four side-facing seats to get one additional forward-facing seat.

2.1.1.6 MTA New York City Transit.

The New York City Transit (NYCT) conducted three studies of customer attitudes toward low-floor buses prior to their purchasing low-floor buses (References 9, 10, and 11). A summary of the findings of each of the studies are given in the following paragraphs.

The objectives of the first study were to obtain customer and bus operator feedback on a low-floor design, perceptions of an ideal bus design, and preferences on features such as seat orientation, hand grips, and handicapped access. Nine focus groups of eight to ten people were used in the study, and included the following:

- Two groups of rush hour customers,
- Two groups of senior citizen customers,
- One group of off-peak non-senior customers,
- One group of wheelchair user customers,
- One group of visually impaired customers, and
- Two groups of bus operators.

The customer groups were conducted on a "walk-through" of a low-floor bus and a current bus used at NYCT. The low-floor bus was a New Flyer Industries D40L with 37 seats (21 forward-facing and 16 side-facing). The current bus was an RTS bus with 40 seats (22 forward-facing and 18 side-facing).

Following each "walk-through," the participants were asked to provide written evaluations and comments on specific features of the buses. Then, they were asked to provide written preferences/comments on entry, flow through the bus, seating, windows, exit door features, ramp, and the overall satisfaction with the bus. Each session ended with a group discussion of their overall reactions to the features of the low-floor bus, their bus experiences, and suggestions for improvements.

The most frequently mentioned concern with respect to riding experience for all groups was crowded conditions (i.e., no seat, no room to stand, etc.). The satisfaction with the low-floor bus was divided. The seniors, young mothers, and people with disabilities generally liked the low-floor bus. Their desire for an easier access outweighed any perceived negatives. However, the rush hour customers preferred the current bus over the low-floor bus. They perceived the low-floor bus to have less room (i.e., less seats and no room to stand) for the rush hour conditions which they face. All groups expressed concerns with the steps up to the rear portion of the low-floor bus.

In the second study, three low-floor buses and a current bus were evaluated by customer groups. The low-floor buses included a New Flyer Industries D40L (39 seats), an Orion Bus Industries Orion VI (28 seats with 21 forward facing and the exit door behind the rear axle), and a hybrid electric bus (33 seats). The customer groups were equally divided between rush hour customers and off-peak customers.

The customer groups were given a 20 minute ride on each of the buses, then asked to fill out a questionnaire. During the test ride, the bus simulated operational service and the wheelchair lift or ramp was demonstrated.

In general, customers were favorable toward the low-floor buses because of the greater ease of entering and exiting the bus. The acceptability of the low-floor buses was conditioned on an acceptable seating capacity and interior configuration. If there were too few seats and a sense of insufficient space to flow through the bus, the current bus was preferred over the low-floor bus.

In the third study, a New Flyer Industries D40L bus (37 seats with 21 forward facing) was tested in revenue service from January to May 1997. A total of 685 customer surveys were distributed, completed, and collected on the bus over three days (March 6 and 13 and May 9). Overall customer reaction was very positive. The customer ratings of the bus features are given in Table 2.7.

2.2 Customer Comfort and Environment Issues

Overall, the transit agencies reported that their customers were pleased with the ease of boarding and were generally satisfied with the comfort and environment of their low-floor buses. The transit agencies also reported that occasional customer complaints have been received on the comfort and environment of their low-floor buses. Some of these complaints result from features inherent in the design of a low-floor bus, such as windows fogging ("can't see out"). Other complaints are more a result that the low-floor bus is a "new bus model," and refinements in its design and development are needed. The most frequent areas cited are discussed in the following sections.

2.2.1 Visibility

Low-floor buses, with their high ceilings, generally have larger windows. The large windows and high ceilings provide the customer with a feeling of spaciousness, which contributes to the comfort of passengers. Also, police officers and transit inspectors like the large windows since they have increased visibility of the inside of the bus.

When the windows are clear, the customers like the larger windows and improved visibility of the low-floor buses. However, road spray and window fogging (in winter) problems can reduce the visibility offered by the larger windows. When the road is wet, slushy, or wet with snow mixed with salt and sand, the road spray can obscure all of the lower portion of the passenger windows from the back of the front wheels to the rear of the bus.

The road spray from the front tires seems to be drawn back to the side of the bus causing the windows (the lower half) to be covered by spray and road grime. Since the windows on a low-floor bus are lower than on a high-floor bus, they are impacted more. The sides of high-floor buses are also covered by road spray, but since the windows are higher from the pavement, the windows are less affected.

Several of the transit agencies have installed an air dam in front of the front axle. The air dam is essentially a "mud flap" that extends the entire width of the bus which

Table 2.7 NYCT Survey Customer Ratings of Features of Low-Floor Buses

Bus Feature	Number	Responses, in Percent of Total		
		Excellent	Satisfactory	Unacceptable
Bus Entrance				
Width of Doors	663	79	20	1
Step Up Into the Bus	622	80	18	3
Overall Ease of Entry	618	79	19	2
Interior of Bus				
Feeling of Enough Space	652	53	34	13
Number of Seats	624	32	50	18
Width of the Aisle at Front of Bus	626	55	34	11
Feeling of Safety in an Accident	590	38	52	10
Feeling of Safety from People Outside the Bus	581	41	52	6
Rear of Bus				
Width of the Aisle at Rear of Bus	628	44	42	14
Seating Arrangement of Rear of Bus	615	48	41	10
Steps in the Aisle	598	39	41	20
This Bus Overall	481	54	37	9

Source: Reference 11

modifies the air flow under the bus. A photo of a low-floor bus equipped with an air dam is shown in Figure 2.1.

The transit agencies reported that the air dam was effective in reducing the road spray on passenger windows. The AATA and CT have replaced the rubber fenders on their front tires with a brush system similar to what is seen on many of the UPS trucks. The CT has both front and rear tires equipped with these brush systems. Both transit agencies reported that the brushes reduced the road spray that would accumulate on the side passenger window. A photo of a front tire of a CT low-floor bus equipped with the brush system is shown in Figure 2.2.

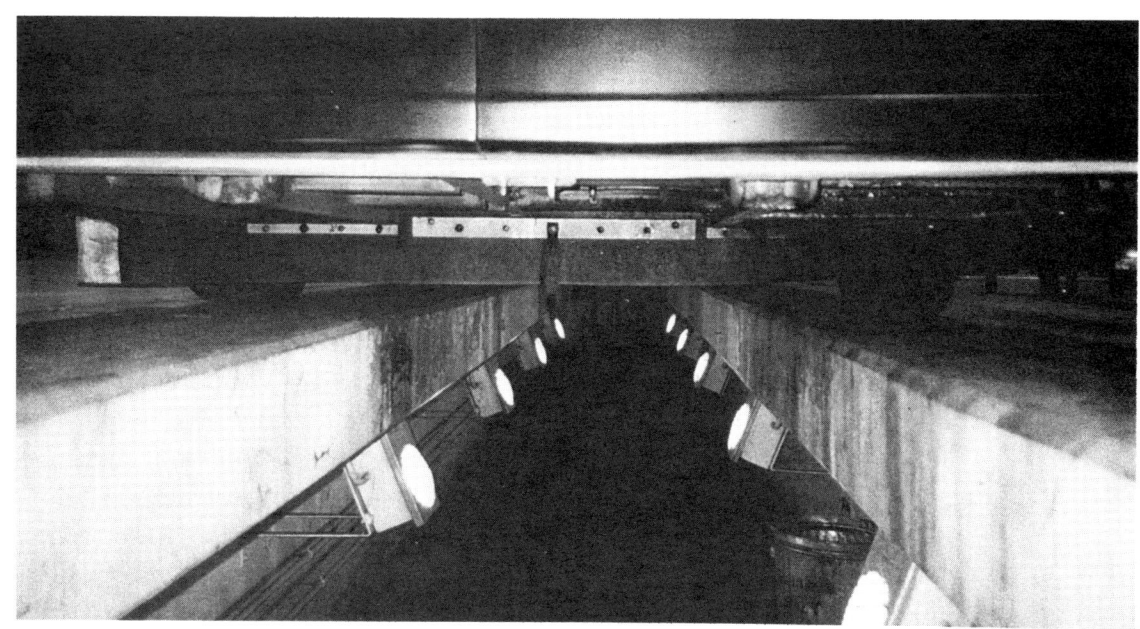

Figure 2.1 Low-Floor Bus Equipped with an Air Dam

Figure 2.2 Calgary Transit Bus with Brush System

Passenger visibility may also be reduced by condensation of water vapor on the windows. CT said that this has been a continuing problem for them with their low-floor buses. Winter in Calgary can be quite variable, cold, snow, sunshine, and warm all in the same day. A lot of salt and sand is used on the streets to keep them safe. As a result, CT buses can become very dirty with slush and road grime during the day. CT buses are washed at the end of the day and stored in a heated garage. When the buses pull out in the early morning, it can be quite cold, and the windows quickly become completely fogged. This problem is compounded by the lack of effective air flow across the windows in low-floor buses.

In high-floor buses, the air vents are below the passenger windows and warm air is directed <u>up</u> across the window. In low-floor buses, the air vents are above the passenger windows, and the warm air is directed <u>down</u> across the windows. This air flow design results in the condensation at the top of the window being removed first, however, that area is generally above a seated passenger's line of sight. Also, it is more difficult to direct an effective stream of warm air down compared with directing a flow of warm air up. In Canada, there are developments underway to achieve a "warm wall" system which will have air vents under the passenger windows. The "warm wall" systems used in their high-floor buses have proven to be effective for their cold climates, but they add to the weight and cost of the bus.

2.2.2 Heating and Ventilation

The heating and ventilation system on a high-floor bus is a hot-water, forced air design which provides a positive air pressure with recirculating fresh and return air. A heater box is mounted under the floor about in the middle of the bus. Duct work running along the walls of the bus at floor level distributes the heated air. In a "warm wall" design, about 20 percent of this heated air is directed up inside the bus wall to vents under the windows which direct warm air across the windows to reduce fogging.

Since the heater box cannot be placed under the floor of a low-floor bus, heating of a low-floor bus is more difficult. The heating and ventilation systems for a low-floor bus are located on the roof or in the rear of the bus above the engine. The warm air is distributed by duct work in the ceiling and directed down across the windows in the passenger compartment. The initial designs of low-floor buses only had the warm air distributed by the ceiling vents. Transit agencies with this type of heating for their low-floor buses received frequent complaints of cold feet from their customers.

In response to these complaints, bus manufacturers added floor area auxiliary heaters which provide forced warm air on both sides of the bus in the floor area. The auxiliary heaters are supplied by hot engine coolant that is pumped through a heat exchanger. In some cases, a booster heater is used to increase the temperatures of the engine coolant. Other designs use a radiant baseboard type system using circulating hot water that is heated by an exchanger which has a heater core with circulating engine coolant. The new heating systems of low-floor buses have resolved the initial problems, and the transit agencies that were interviewed were generally satisfied with the comfort of their buses in winter conditions. However, some transit agencies located in very cold climates are still requesting a "warm wall" design.

2.2.2.1 Urban Bus Ventilation and Climate Control Study. As a part of a study on bus ventilation and climate control by the Canadian Urban Transit Association (CUTA) and Transport Canada, a series of tests were conducted to measure the performance of the ventilation and heating systems on urban buses (References 24 and 25). The test measurements included airflows in the passenger and operator areas, temperature measurements in the passenger and operator areas, and air patterns. Tests were conducted on all three low-floor buses made by Canadian bus manufacturers. Tests were also conducted on conventional high-floor models for comparison purposes. The key findings of these tests are discussed in the following paragraphs.

The ASHRAE Standard for "Ventilation for Acceptable Indoor Air Quality" recommends a minimum make up air (MUA) for transportation vehicles of 15 cubic feet per minute (cfm) per occupant (Reference 19). Only one low-floor bus met the ASHRAE Standard when using only the passenger system on high-speed setting. All but one met the ASHRAE Standard when both the operator and passenger systems were on high-speed settings. None of the high-floor buses tested met the ASHRAE Standard when using both the passenger and the operator systems on high-speed settings.

The temperature measurements found rather large temperature differentials in the buses tested indicating some shortcomings of the air distribution within the buses. The measured horizontal temperature differentials for the head zone level ranged from 8°F to 17°F, and for the foot zone level ranged from 10°F to 23°F. The vertical temperature differentials ranged from 6°F to 20°F.

The ASHRAE Standard for "Thermal Environmental Conditions for Human Occupancy" recommends an optimum temperature of 71°F and a temperature range of 68°F to 75°F for people dressed in typical indoor winter clothing (Reference 20). None of the low-floor buses tested met this temperature range. The observed temperature range for the head zone level was 63°F to 88°F. The ASHRAE Standard 55-1992 also recommends a head to foot temperature differential of no greater than 5°F. None of the low-floor buses tested met the recommended vertical temperature differentials for all areas of the bus. A new ventilation and climate control system specification is being developed by CUTA to address these issues.

2.2.3 *Dust Intrusion*

Several of the transit agencies reported higher levels of dust intrusion in their low-floor buses compared with their conventional buses. The Phoenix Transit System (PTS) said that an investigation conducted for them suggested that the dust was entering through the doors. Once inside, the dust would be sucked into the air recirculation system and distributed throughout the bus.

The MTA had problems with dust intrusion in their low-floor buses. The MTA devised a smoke bomb test to identify how the dust entered the buses. A smoke bomb was placed on a bracket in the right upper corner of the rear mounted air-conditioning (AC) unit. The bracket was the normal storage place for their wheel shocks. The smoke bomb was set off with the bus stationary. No intrusion of smoke into the passenger compartment was observed. The MTA test personnel decided to drive the bus. No smoke inside the bus was observed until the speed was about 20 mph. Then, so much smoke had entered the interior of the bus that the test driver could not see and stopped the bus. Smoke passed through the rear bulkhead and entered the plenum area between the roof and ceiling, and then entered the passenger compartment. The rear bulkhead has several electrical and tubing penetrations. Also, the multiplex controller with many wires is in the same general area. The MTA staff were uncertain as to the paths for the smoke penetration to the bus interior, but hypothesized that the passenger compartment built up a negative pressure as the bus moved, and at 20 mph, the negative pressure was high enough to cause the smoke to enter through the plenum area into the interior of the bus. The perception of the MTA staff was that dust enters the bus in a similar manner, and is distributed throughout the bus by the air recirculation system. The pressure inside the bus was not measured during the tests. Therefore, no direct confirmation of their hypothesis was made. However, the MTA staff also noted that buses operating in the central business district (CBD) where exhaust fumes are relatively high, frequently report entry of exhaust fumes inside their buses. These observations tend to support their hypothesis that their low-floor buses develop negative pressures in the interior of the bus as they move. The MTA low-floor buses do not have a separate fresh air intake in their climate control system. The MTA feels that sufficient outside air will enter through the doorways at the frequent stops along the route.

The Capital District Transportation Authority (CDTA) also reported excessive dust in the rear third of their low-floor buses. The exit door on the CDTA low-floor buses is behind the rear axle. The CDTA staff thought that dust enters their bus when the rear door is opened at stops. The CDTA low-floor buses do not have a separate fresh air intake in their climate control system. Fresh air enters the bus when the doors are opened at the stops.

2.2.4 Noise and Vibration

Several of the transit agencies said that they have received some customer complaints related to the noise and vibrations of low-floor buses. Occasional complaints were received about vibration on the low-floor buses powered with a four cylinder engine. These complaints usually come from customers seated in the rear of the bus.

CT conducted interior and exterior noise tests of their low-floor and high-floor buses. The results of these tests are given in Table 2.8. As can be seen in Table 2.8, the tests found that the low-floor buses generally had higher interior noise levels for both the passenger and operator areas. However, the test measurements of the exterior noise levels resulted in mixed findings relative to low-floor buses compared to high-floor buses. It is of interest to note that the newer low-floor bus (1995) with the 50 Series engine had lower exterior noise level measurements than any of the high-floor buses tested.

Table 2.8 Interior and Exterior Noise Levels of Calgary Transit Buses, Accelerating From 0 to 35 mph

Bus Model	Engine (Fuel)	Interior Noise Level in dB(A)				Exterior Noise in dB(A)	
		Front	Middle	Rear	Driver	Curb Side	Street Side
New Flyer Industries, D40L -- 1993(*)	6V92TA (Diesel)	81.2	83.1	82.5	80.4	81.8	81.5
New Flyer Industries, D40L -- 1995(*)	50 Series (Diesel)	77.6	78.5	84.4	81.4	75.9	77.2
New Flyer Industries, D40 -- 1991	6V92TA (Diesel)	74.5	74.2	83.1	72.1	80.7	80.8
MCI, Classic -- 1992	6V92TA (Diesel)	71.3	71.0	79.1	71.4	79.7	81.0
Orion Bus Industries, Orion V -- 1982	6V71 (Diesel)	73.2	74.6	77.4	71.4	84.0	82.8
New Flyer, D 901 -- 1982	6V71 (Diesel)	76.0	78.5	82.8	73.9	79.7	81.0
GMC, 5307 -- 1982	6V71 (Diesel)	75.0	76.3	82.3	74.8	79.3	81.8

Source: Calgary Transit

TEST procedures are based on SAE J366b.

(*) Low-floor buses, all other buses are high-floor.

Two of the tests conducted on buses at the Altoona Bus Testing Center (ABTC) are exterior noise and interior noise. Table 2.9 gives the test results of seven low-floor and four high-floor buses that have been tested by the ABTC. As can be seen in Table 2.9, the passenger, operator, or exterior noise level measurements indicate mixed findings between low-floor buses and high-floor buses. These tests appear to indicate that there are no consistent and significant differences in the noise levels of low-floor and high-floor buses.

2.2.5 Ride Quality

Several of the transit agencies said that customers had complained about the smoothness of the ride and the harshness of the brakes on their low-floor buses. Neither of these issues appear to be inherent to a low-floor bus design, but seem to be more an issue of improving the control and coordination of the power train and braking systems during acceleration and deceleration. Adjustments in brake balance and retarder control and operator training and experience were reported by some transit agencies as improving the ride quality and reducing the number of customer complaints. Some transit agencies are working with their bus manufacturer to improve the control and coordination of the transmission, engine, and retarder systems.

2.3 Capacity and Ridership Impacts

A major concern about low-floor buses is vehicle capacity, and the possible impacts concerning the number of buses required for a given route. The maximum number of passengers that can be serviced by a bus route is a function of the capacity of the buses operating on the line and the average headway between the buses on the line. A general discussion of the factors impacting the number of passengers that can be carried on a line is given in Appendix B. If the loading standard calls for a seat for every expected customer, then the number of seats on a bus is the capacity of that bus. If the loading standard permits standees, then the capacity of the bus is a function of the combination of seats and the number of standees that the bus can carry. The capacities of the low-floor buses that were in operation at the transit agencies interviewed are discussed in a following section on Vehicle Capacity.

The number of buses needed to be assigned to a route, for a given headway, is inversely proportional to the average speed that can be maintained along the route. Therefore, to be able to carry more passengers on a route for a given bus capacity, and not increase the number of buses assigned to the route, the average speed along the route must be increased. The methods to increase speed along a route could include: use of an exclusive bus lane, bus priority at intersections, and decrease in dwell times.

Low-floor buses offer the potential to reduce dwell times through faster boarding and alighting times. However, only a fraction of the dwell time is consumed by boardings and alightings. A larger portion of dwell time is composed of fare collection, re-entry of bus from a stop zone into the traffic lane, and the operator answering passenger questions. The boarding and alighting times for ambulatory and disabled passengers for both low-floor and high-floor buses are given in the following section.

Table 2.9 Noise Levels of Transit Buses Measured at Altoona, Accelerating from 0 to 35 mph

Bus Model	Engine (Fuel)	Interior Noise Level in dB(A)				Exterior Noise in dB(A)	
		Front	Middle	Rear	Driver	Curb Side	Street Side
Gillig Corporation, Low-Floor Bus(*)	Cum M11 (Diesel)	74.4	74.0	77.3	73.5	74.0	75.4
Neoplan, AN 440L(*)	DDC 50 (Diesel)	74.1	75.6	76.9	73.7	81.8	76.7
New Flyer Industries, D40L(*)	DDC 6V92TA (Diesel)	76.9	77.0	79.8	75.2	71.45	72.95
New Flyer Industries, D40L(*)	DDC 50 (Diesel)	73.5	74.2	76.5	72.1	77.8	77.6
Nova Bus, LFS(*)	Cum 8.3 (Diesel)	80.5	81.6	82.3	77.8	78.7	83.9
Orion Bus Industries, Orion VI(*)	Cum L-10 (CNG)	74.2	78.2	80.5	72.8	83.1	85.6
New Flyer Industries, D40	DDC 50 (CNG)	73.9	75.6	78.0	75.1	73.0	74.7
Nova Bus, Classic	DDC 50 (Diesel)	74.5	76.9	80.0	72.8	76.6	74.2
Nova Bus, RTS	Cum L-10 (CNG)	76.3	75.5	79.5	75.7	75.4	80.2
Orion Bus Industries, Orion V	Cum L-10 (CNG)	69.8	72.9	77.4	69.1	75.0	76.8

Source: Altoona Bus Test Reports

TEST procedures are based on SAE J366b for the exterior noise measurements and White Book for the interior noise measurements.

(*)Low-floor bus, all other buses are high-floor.

2.3.1 Boarding and Alighting Times

There is some thought that more rapid boarding and alighting times of a low-floor bus might lead to shorter dwell times and faster schedule speeds. No original data on boarding and alighting times were collected during this study. However, there were four references found in the literature that did contain information on boarding and alighting times (References 1, 13, 26, and 27). None of these references provide information on any changes in running times. The boarding and alighting times for ambulatory passengers from five transit agencies are given in Table 2.10. The data for Vancouver and Victoria were obtained from the observations of a large number of boarding and alighting in revenue service (over 14,000 and 4,000 respectively). The boarding times given for Ann Arbor were for two types of service, revenue and shuttle. The revenue service times were mean boarding times for cash and no cash (pass or prepaid media) transactions. The shuttle service times were observed during a Summer Art Fair, where fares were collected prior to boarding and all doors were used. The times for Kitchner Transit and St. Albert Transit were boarding and alighting times measured during revenue service.

In August of 1996, the Paralympics were held in Atlanta. The U.S. Department of Transportation's Volpe National Transportation Systems Center (VNTSC) conducted a limited operational assessment of the specialized transportation service that was provided for the athletes participating in the event (Reference 27). A specific focus of the assessment was the bus access technologies that enabled boarding and alighting of the athletes using mobility aids. As a part of this assessment, a number of measurements of the boarding and alighting times were made. The results of ramp and lift boarding and alighting time measurements are given in Table 2.11. The ramps were New Flyer Industries and the lifts were Lift-U™. A caution needs to be made that because of possible differences in the transportation services provided and the capabilities of the athletes, the observed boarding and alighting times may not be realized in typical transit operations. These data were the only statistical data found on the boarding and alighting times for passengers using wheelchairs.

It should be pointed out that the total dwell time of a bus in revenue service would include: time to maneuver to a securement location and time to secure the mobility aid. These times were not reported. Many of the athletes did not use the securements. Also, it needs to be pointed out that many of the wheelchairs were the long tri-wheeled competition type, and this could have impacted the times.

The report cited three advantages of low-floor buses equipped with ramps. First, boarding and alighting are not disrupted by a failure of the ramp. Second, non-disabled persons could more easily access the bus. Third, only one deployment/stowage cycle of a ramp is required, irrespective of the number of boarding or alighting persons with mobility aids.

2.3.2 Vehicle Capacity

In general, all of the low-floor buses currently offered to transit agencies will have fewer seats than a same-size high-floor model. This is because of the loss of usable floor area to mount seats because of the

Table 2.10 Average Boarding and Alighting Times for Ambulatory Passengers

Transit Agency	Boarding Times (Seconds)		Alighting Times (Seconds)	
	Low-Floor	High-Floor	Low-Floor	High-Floor
Ann Arbor Transportation Authority				
Revenue: Cash	3.09	3.57	1.32[a]	2.55[a]
No Cash	1.92	2.76	2.17[b]	2.67[b]
Shuttle: No Fare	1.91	2.26	Not Reported	Not Reported
Victoria Regional Transit System	3.02	3.78	1.87[a] 2.13[b]	3.61[a] 1.84[b]
Vancouver Regional Transit System	Not Applicable	3.78	Not Applicable	2.62[a] 1.43[b]
St. Albert Transit				
Single Boarding	3.61	4.27	Not Reported	Not Reported
Two Boarding	6.15	7.27		
Senior Boarding	3.88	6.10		
Kitchner Transit	2.23	2.42	1.16	1.49

Sources: References 1, 13 and 26

---

[a] Front door.
[b] Rear door.

intrusion of the wheel wells, and sometimes the engine compartment, into the passenger cabin. The loss per wheel well has been estimated to be three seats (Reference 13).

In Europe, seats mounted on platforms and rear-facing seats are accepted, so the number of seats lost on their low-floor buses is less. These practices are generally not used in North America. Seats that face to the rear, and in particular, those that cause a passenger to have a close proximity to another passenger looking at them are not popular with North American passengers. The PTS had such a situation with their first order of low-floor buses. A row of rear-facing seats was placed on the rear side of the front wheel wells. The next row of seats was front-facing. The spacing between the front edges of the seats was about seventeen inches. The PTS received many customer complaint concerning these seats, both that they were rear-facing and too close. In the second order of low-floor bus, the row of rear-facing seats was replaced with a single

Table 2.11 Measurements of the Deploy/Stow and Boarding/Alighting Times For Ramp and Lift Operations During the Paralympics

Operation	Time in Seconds
Mean Time to Deploy Ramp (powered operation)	10.5 (6)[a]
Mean Time to Deploy Ramp (manual operation)	7.6 (2)
Mean Time to Deploy Lift (for boarding, out and down)	10.6 (63)
Mean Time to Deploy Lift (for alighting, out and up)	10.4 (27)
Mean Time to Board -- Ramp	6.3 (7)
Mean Cycle-Time to Board or Alight -- Lift	24.4 (16)
Mean Time to Alight -- Ramp	[b]
Mean Time to Stow -- Ramp (powered operation)	10.6 (8)
Mean Time to Stow -- Ramp (manual operation)	8.8 (2)
Mean Time to Stow -- Lift	11.5 (7)

Sources: Reference 27

---

[a] Number of observations in sample.
[b] Times not reported.

---

aisle-facing seat on each side. The original order of low-floor buses was retrofitted with the same seating arrangement. The MTA's customer survey found a similar customer preference (Reference 8). Also, the MTA survey revealed that their customers strongly preferred front-facing seats. They were willing to give up almost four aisle-facing seats to get one additional front-facing seat.

The number of seats lost depends on the usable floor space in the bus and the seating arrangement chosen by the transit agency. Some transit agencies try to maximize the number of seats in their buses, and others try to maximize the number of passengers that their buses can carry. Each have valid reasons for their decision because of the different types of service that they are providing to their customers. Examples of this difference in choice of seating arrangements by transit agencies are shown in Table 2.12. Also, as shown in Table 2.12, the maximum number of seats (assuming the use of only front-facing or aisle facing seats) for 40-foot, low-floor buses ranges from 31 to 40. Table 2.13 provides the same

Table 2.12 Passenger Capacities of 40-Foot, Low-Floor Buses with Two Wheelchair Positions

Manufacturer, Model		Number of Seats	Capacity with Standees	Source
Gillig -- Low Floor Bus		40[a]	87[b]	GIL
Neoplan USA -- AN440L		40[a]	54[b]	NEO
New Flyer Industries --	D40L	39	70	CTA
	D40L	38	66	PTS
	D40L	39	64	MCTS
	C40L	40[a]	60	MARTA
North American Bus Industries --	40LFW	39	59[c]	NABI
Nova Bus --	LFS	39[d]	65[d]	STCUM
	LFS	31[d]	80[d]	STCUM
Orion Bus Industries --	ORION VI	32	48	CDTA
	ORION VI	35[a]	75	OBI

[a] Maximum number of seats, as advertised in manufacturers promotional material.
[b] Capacity estimate by formula, (GVWR-CW) 150.
[c] Manufacturer used number of standees as 50% of number of seats.
[d] Seating arrangement has rear-facing seats and only one wheelchair position.

Table 2.13 Passenger Capacities of 40-Foot, High-Floor Buses with Two Wheelchair Positions

Manufacturer, Model	Maximum No. of Seats[a]	Capacity with Standees	Source
Gillig -- Phantom	45	69	GIL
Neoplan USA -- AN440	45	78	NEO
New Flyer Industries -- D40	45	85	NFIL
North American Bus Industries	43	65	NABI
Nova Bus (TMC) -- RTS	44	74	PTS
Orion Bus Industries -- Orion V	45	85	MCTS

Source: Bus Manufacturers

[a] All seats are forward or aisle facing.

information for 40-foot, high-floor buses, where the maximum number of seats ranges from 43 to 45. It should be noted that in some cases, spacing between seats may be affected in order to achieve high seat capacity.

If a transit agency's loading standard is to provide a seat for each expected customer, then the loss of passenger capacity on a route would be directly proportional to the reduction in the number of seats on the bus, assuming no changes in the schedule speed or headway. Assuming no changes in frequency of service (headway) or schedule speed, the transit agency would have to add buses (with operators) to provide the same number of seats for their customers. In a recent bus procurement by King County Department of Transportation/Metro (Seattle), the authority decided to purchase high-floor buses rather than low-floor buses. The main reason given was because of the loss of seats with the low-floor model, and the cost implications that it would have.

2.3.3 *Experiences of Interviewed Transit Agencies*

In the interviews with transit agencies, two of the transit agencies said that the lower capacity of their low-floor buses would probably require adding more buses on routes to maintain their service standards, and one was evaluating their situation. Table 2.14 shows the responses that were given by the transit agencies. As can be seen in Table 2.14, for most of the interviewed agencies their low-floor fleet represents 25 percent or less of their active fleet. Three agencies have low-floor fleets that are approximately one-half of their active fleet. Therefore, none could report on experience of an all low-floor fleet for peak period operations. Several had routes with all low-floor buses for off-peak periods. However, capacity is not an issue during those periods.

For the cases of Calgary Transit (CT) and Victoria Regional Transit System (VRTS), their ridership has been increasing rapidly, and they have had to add buses to routes to accommodate the increase in ridership. Both agencies thought that some of the requirements for more buses might have been caused by the lower capacity of their low-floor buses. Neither had conducted an analysis of their data to determine whether or not their perceptions were correct. The experiences of the CTA and the STCUM are discussed more completely in the following sections.

2.3.3.1 Chicago Transit Authority. The CTA has established Service Standards for both bus and rail operations which define the loading standards that apply for various types of service such as "crosstown" and "downtown" (Reference 11). In rush hours, the objective is to serve all passengers, while minimizing the use of buses and operators. During the "peak of the peak," rapid transit feeder and downtown routes are scheduled for about 70 passengers per standard 40-foot bus. Crosstown routes are scheduled for up to 65 passengers per standard 40-foot bus. At other times of the day buses are scheduled to provide seats for all passengers to improve service marketability and since the cost of using buses and labor is less relative to peak hour service. For example, during weekday midday periods and for weekends, loads of up to 45 passengers per standard 40-foot bus are permitted. During the "evening" and "owl" periods, the loading standard is relaxed even more to maintain reasonable wait times for passengers.

Table 2.14 Capacity Impacts with Low-Floor Buses

Transit Agency	Low-Floor Fleet as percentage of Active Fleet	Change in Number of Buses Required on Routes with Low-Floor Buses	No. of Seats on Low-Floor Buses	Capacity with Standees	
				Low-Floor[a]	High-Floor[a]
Ann Arbor Transportation Authority	62	No	36	56	57
BC Transit - Victoria Regional Transit System	42	Possibly	36 38	[b]	[b]
Calgary Transit	26	Possibly	36 39	65	75[c]
Capital District Transportation Authority	9	No	32	48	75
Champaign-Urbana Mass Transit District	55	No	36	61	71
Chicago Transit Authority	3	No	39	70	70
Metropolitan Atlanta Rapid Transit Authority	24	No	40 39	60 59	71
Milwaukee County Transit System	26	No	39	64	70
Phoenix Transit System	27	No	37	65	74
Société de Transport de la Communauté Urbaine de Montréal	17	To Be Determined[d]	39 31	65 80[e]	80[c]
Société de Transport de la Rive-Sud de Montréal	8	No	38	65	Information Not Available

(a) With two wheelchair positions, except where noted.
(b) The Victoria Regional Transit System does not use a specific capacity number for their buses.
(c) Calgary Transit and STCUM high-floor buses do not carry passengers in wheelchairs.
(d) STCUM is testing new seating configuration that would keep low-floor bus "natural" capacity the same as conventional STUCM buses.
(e) STCUM low-floor buses have one wheelchair position.

An appendix to the Service Standards entitled, "Frequency Guidelines Working Paper" provides guidelines for determining frequency of service based on passenger volumes observed at a route's maximum load point, or points. Checks are taken at these points approximately eight times in a year. Using the maximum load point data ensures that adequate service is scheduled to accommodate all expected passengers by adjusting the headway and the number of buses scheduled. The highest required capacity for a 40-foot bus is 70 passengers as discussed in the previous paragraph. The CTA believes that their low-floor buses with the seating arrangement that was chosen meet that requirement. The seating arrangement for the CTA low-floor buses is shown in Figure 2.3.

One of the CTA routes that has low-floor buses assigned to it is the "Number 151 Sheridan Route." The Sheridan Route has high passenger loads with frequent stops, and is an example of operating experience with a mix of low-floor and high-floor buses on a route. Only accessible buses are scheduled on the route. The mix of low- and high-floor buses varies on the availability of buses for pullout. A description of the route follows.

The Sheridan Route is one of the older routes in Chicago. It was begun in March 1917 by the Chicago Motor Bus Company. The route follows along the lake shore, and provides 24-hour accessible service between the Devon/Clark terminals in the North and the Union Station in the downtown area. The route provides accessible service to residents living in the apartments and homes along the lake shore.

The route is 10.5 miles long with frequent stops (about every block), and has a weekday ridership of over 22,000. The minimum headway is approximately two minutes during the peak periods, and drops off to about a six minute headway during the base period. The schedule speed during the peak periods is about 8 mph. The route has 49 buses assigned for the weekday peak periods, and 21 buses for the weekday base periods. The one hour passenger volume at the maximum load point is 1,583 which occurs during the AM peak period. The average bus loading during this one-hour period is 45 passengers. The CTA staff reported that no changes in the number of buses assigned or changes in the service schedule have been made with the use of low-floor buses on the route.

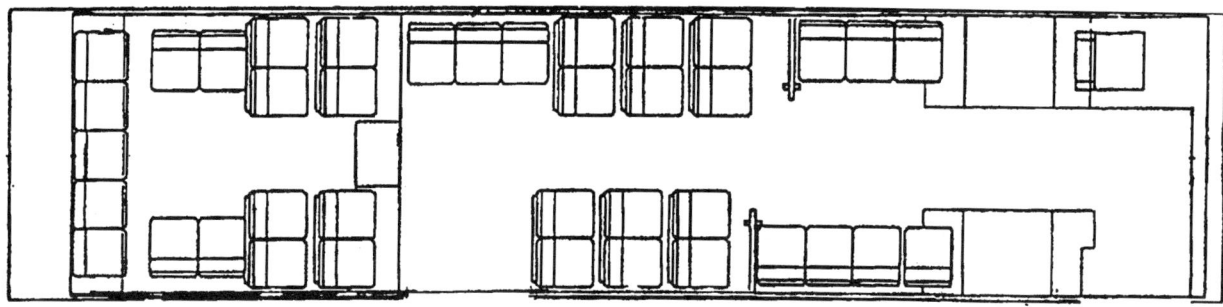

Figure 2.3 Seating Arrangement for the CTA Low-Floor Bus

2.3.3.2 Société de Transport de la Communauté Urbaine de Montréal. The reasons for the initial customer dissatisfaction at the STCUM appear to stem from difficulties in passenger flow and congestion within the bus, and a change in the exit door activation. The major concerns centered on passenger flow and congestion in the area of the front wheelhouses and between the two doors, the exit door, and in accessing the seats to the extreme rear of the bus. It needs to be pointed out that STCUM had much heavier passenger loads (an average of 54.58 passengers per vehicle-hour) than any of the other agencies interviewed (see Table 2.1). The congestion experienced at STCUM may not occur at lower passenger loads.

A plan view of the interior design is given in Figure 2.4. A two-one seating arrangement was selected between the doors to provide both seating and total capacities comparable to their regular high-floor bus. One of the goals of the design was to maximize the number of seats in spite of the room taken up inside the bus by the wheelhouses. A photo of the interior of the bus is shown in Figure 2.5.

During rush hour, crowding, particularly in the front of the bus, would occur, obstructing passengers from moving to seats in the rear of the bus. Several factors seem to contribute to the restricted flow. The area around the front wheelhouses is an attractive place to stop, put bags and parcels on and to lean on, thus, constricting the aisle for flow of passengers to the rear of the bus. Occasionally, passengers would sit on top of the wheel wells with feet in the aisle, further obstructing it. As can be seen in Figures 2.5 and 2.6, there are three areas with aisle facing seats. Customers have their feet in the aisle, and occasionally have packages in the aisle. Also, shown in Figure 2.5 is a safety stanchion for the compartment for wheelchair customers which is located in the aisle directly in front of the center exit door. This stanchion attracts standing passengers restricting easy passenger flow to the back of the bus and access to the exit door. All of these factors tended to impede the flow of passengers to the rear of the bus.

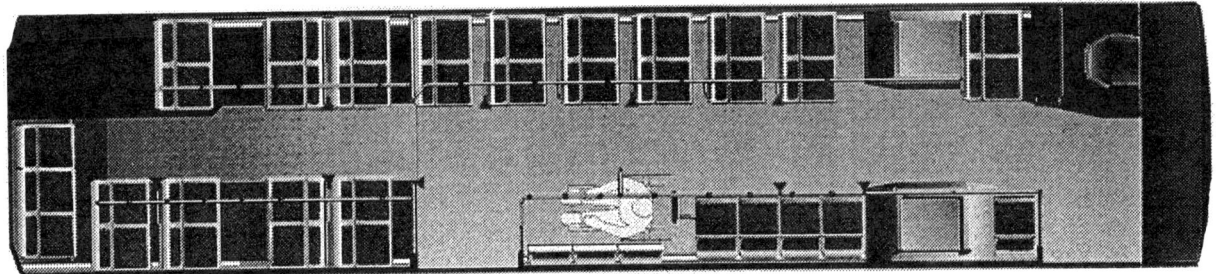

Figure 2.4 Original Interior Design of Low-Floor Buses for STCUM
Source: STCUM

Figure 2.5 Photo of the Interior Design of Low-Floor Buses for STCUM
Source: STCUM

In addition, there was a tendency for passengers to attempt to exit from the front door rather than the rear door, which compounded the problem. The reasons for this behavior are not fully understood. One factor may be the change in how a passenger would activate the center exit door. For the last twenty years, passengers had become familiar with "McKay" push gates and treadles to activate the center exit door. The low-floor buses have a motion detector mounted above the door to sense the presence of an exiting passenger. In addition, the maximum speed safety standard before opening a door has been reduced from 3 mph to 1 mph. Passenger unfamiliarity with the door control and the new safety standard resulted in door opening delay, occasionally resulting in a customer complaint to the driver. As a result, many passengers would try to exit from the front door.

The crowding of passengers in the front of the bus gives the impression that the bus is full, and customers are left at the curb when there is still room in the rear of the bus. While most passengers appreciate the ease of boarding and the modern looks, they are not happy with the crowded interior.

The STCUM uses a computer simulation for analyzing scheduling requirements. The model determines the number of buses required to meet expected customer ons and offs along a route for various service frequencies and bus passenger capacities. The original interior design of the STCUM low-floor bus had 39 seats and a single wheelchair position. The "natural" capacity (normal standee load, not crush load) of this bus was 65 passengers. Their current high-floor buses with no wheelchair positions have a "natural" capacity of 80 passengers. This reduction in passenger capacity would have resulted in a significant increase in the number of buses required for a given route if all buses were low-floor. However, the STCUM is evaluating two new interior designs, each with only 31 seats that have a "natural" capacity of 80, which is the same as their current buses. While the new interior design provides an equivalent vehicle capacity as their current high-floor buses, there are 24 percent fewer seats (31 versus 41). Twenty low-floor buses with these new interior designs are currently under evaluation in revenue service.

The STCUM and their bus manufacturer are jointly working to test a number of seating options and modifications to improve passenger acceptance. A signal was added and new operating instructions posted to provide an exiting passenger a positive indication of how and when the door may be opened. To facilitate passenger flow, seven seats have been removed to open up the interior of the bus. Two new interior designs are under consideration. The seating arrangement is the same for both; refer to Figure 2.6 for the new seating arrangement. The difference between the two designs is in the access to the rear seats. One has a slope in the aisle to clear the rear axle, and the other uses steps in the aisle. The new interior design opens up the aisle for easier movement within the bus and also increases the area for standees. Twenty low-floor buses with these new interior designs are currently under evaluation in revenue service.

2.4 Impacts on Ridership

Most of the transit agencies report that overall their customers liked the low-floor buses, and several agencies believed that the introduction of low-floor buses has had a positive impact on their ridership. Only three of the transit agencies interviewed have low-floor fleets that are nearly one-half of their active fleet (See Table 2.14). All three said that they feel that the low-floor buses have contributed to an increase in riders, but none had analysis to support their perceptions. The other transit agencies interviewed had low-floor fleets that were twenty-five percent or less of their active fleet, and it would be difficult to evaluate the impacts on ridership at this stage of deployment.

A manager at the Champaign-Urbana Mass Transit District (MTD) said that "...from a passenger standpoint it (*referring to low-floor bus*) is all win." The MTD said that they were experiencing an increase in their "community" riders since the introduction of low-floor buses. These are the riders that are other than the university riders. During the off-peak periods, the MTD community service routes have nearly all low-floor buses assigned. The MTD staff felt that some of the increase was due to the use of low-floor buses, but had not done an analysis to support their perception. The MTD low-floor fleet is about 55 percent of their active fleet.

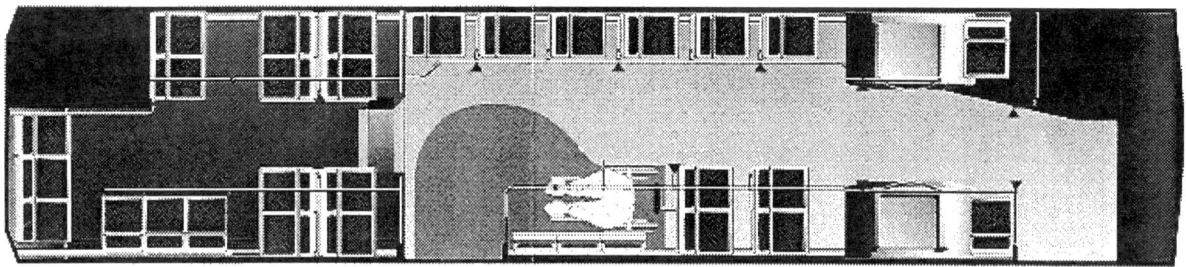

**Figure 2.6 New Interior Design of the STCUM Low-Floor Bus
Source: STCUM**

Several of the transit agencies felt that they could attract more use of fixed-route service by senior and disabled customers with the low-floor service. CT reported a large increase in ridership with the introduction of accessible service on their system (rail and bus). They first introduced accessible service in the Fall of 1993 with low-floor buses and accessible rail stations. The number of wheelchair customers for the next ten months averaged about 162 trips per month. Ridership counts in 1997 show an increase in the average weekly wheelchair trips to approximately 2,900 trips per week. The CT has also seen an increase of persons with canes and walkers using their system. The CT experienced about a six percent growth in total system ridership during the past year, and they anticipate a total of 64.4 million linked trips in 1997.

A separate service for people with disabilities is provided by the City of Calgary called the "Handi-Bus." A survey of <u>ambulatory</u> Handi-Bus customers in March 1997 found about 75 percent were aware of the CT low-floor bus service, and 35 percent of the respondents said that there was a low-floor bus route near their home (22 percent answered that there was no service). Twenty-seven percent of the respondents said that they had used the low-floor or C-Train (Calgary rail) service in the past six months. Forty percent had made ten or more trips, and sixty percent had made five or less trips using the low-floor buses.

A survey of <u>non-ambulatory</u> Handi-Bus customers during the same time found that 76 percent were aware of the low-floor bus service, and 37 percent of the respondents said that a low-floor bus route was near their home (21 percent answered that there was no service). Of the 12 percent of the respondents that had used the low-floor bus or C-Train service in the past six months, 50 percent of the low-floor bus users had made five or less trips, and 25 percent had made ten or more trips.

CT could not specifically quantify the increase of ridership with the introduction of low-floor buses to their fleet, but they did feel that it had contributed. Certainly, the increases in ridership of people with disabilities are directly related to the introduction of accessible service with low-floor buses, and making the C-Train accessible.

The AATA offers a number of accessible services for customers that use a wheelchair or scooter, have trouble walking, have trouble with climbing stairs, have a visual impairment, or some other qualifying disability. In an attempt to attract those customers to the AATA accessible fixed-route service, a test with free fares for passengers with disabilities for a month was conducted during August 1995 followed by a return to charging fares. The hope was that some customers would continue to use the fixed-route service. There was an increase of 183 percent in rides during the test month, and 30 percent increase in riders for the following six months after fares were again charged.

A decision was made to return to free fares for persons with disabilities using the fixed-route service in April 1996. The number of rides on the fixed-route service by customers with disabilities increased over the following 15 months to an average of 13,437 compared to the average of 3,734 before the free fare experiment was conducted (an increase of 260 percent). An AATA analysis indicated that the free fares generated about 64,000 new fixed-route rides per year by persons with disabilities.

The AATA estimated the annual cost savings due to this shift to be slightly over $192,000 (Reference 28).

While the experiment at the AATA cannot be totally attributed to the use of low-floor buses, the shift of customers from their specialized service to their fixed-route service was likely aided by the use of low-floor buses. The AATA active fixed-route fleet is about 60 percent low-floor. For the off-peak periods, the AATA fixed-route service is essentially all low-floor.

2.5 Vehicle Operating Experiences

All of the transit agencies were satisfied with the road clearance attributes of their low-floor buses. The MARTA staff indicated that there were a couple routes with high at-grade railroad crossings on which they did not schedule their low-floor buses. Several of the agencies operating low-floor buses also said that the ramp mechanism protective skid would occasionally ground at steep entrance driveways. The side skirts of all of the low-floor buses that were observed at the transit agencies were approximately 4 to 5 inches closer to the street level than high-floor buses at those agencies. As can be seen in Table 4.1, the breakover angle claimed by most bus manufacturers for their low-floor models is 9.5 to 10°. The NFIL D40L has a breakover angle of 8.3°.

In general, the operators liked the handling qualities of their low-floor bus. The low-floor bus was quicker and had good steering and handling characteristics. Several of the agencies reported a high number of wheels hitting a curb during a right turn. A part of this problem was due to differences in how the low-floor bus would track in making a right turn. At some systems, this problem was corrected by providing additional training for the operators in the proper procedure for making right turns with the new low-floor buses. The CTA corrected this problem by cutting back the curbs or by adding spacers to prevent the wheels from coming in contact with the high curbs. The Milwaukee County Transit System (MCTS) also experienced a high number of wheel hits with their low-floor buses. Their solution, in addition to operator training, was to replace the 275/70R tires with larger 305/70R tires. The MCTS said that with the change in tires, the problem was solved.

The CDTA reported some steering problems during an early heavy, wet snow with their low-floor buses. Some of the moving steering linkages pass through the underfloor structure on the CDTA buses. These linkages were exposed to the weather. During the storm, snow and ice collected and became packed around the steering linkages and in the frame members restricting the operator's ability to steer the bus. The CDTA removed the buses from service for the remainder of the snow storm. The manufacturer developed a fix for the problem consisting of two flaps (similar to mud flaps) that protect the structure in the area of the wheel wells from snow and slush spraying from the tire. The steering linkages pass through cuts in the flap. The CDTA has had several heavy, wet snows since the flaps have been installed, and they reported that the problem appears to be fixed.

2.6 Impacts on Maintenance and Facilities

2.6.1 Maintenance Experiences

Overall, the maintenance experiences with low-floor buses at the transit agencies interviewed have been positive. Many of the early problems experienced by the agencies appear to be problems related to the introduction of a "new" bus, rather than problems intrinsically related to a low-floor design. The causes for these initial problems appear to have been mostly related to production and design issues.

Three low-floor maintenance issues were consistently reported by the transit agencies as being significantly different (better or worse) in comparison to their current high-floor buses. These were: service interruption experiences (road calls) with ramps and lifts, tire life, and brake life.

2.6.1.1 Experiences with Ramps. Probably the most distinguishing feature between a low-floor bus and a high-floor bus is the difference in boarding/alighting, in that there are no steps for ambulatory passengers, and a ramp rather than a lift is used for passengers in wheelchairs. The operating experiences with the ramp versus a lift has been universally positive. The Canadian transit agencies interviewed did not operate lift equipped, high-floor, 40-foot buses. The U.S. transit agencies that had experiences with lift equipped buses reported that service interruptions because of ramp failures either had not occurred or were rare. The PTS said that the road calls for lifts were five to six times more frequent than road calls due to ramp failures. The PTS reported that miles-between-road calls for lifts were 43,500 miles compared to 250,000 miles-between-road calls for ramps. The VRTS reported that 600,000 miles-between-road calls for ramps had been their experience. Other agencies that did not track road calls by these categories reported their experiences with road calls because of ramps as none or very rare.

Lift failure is a major cause of road calls for many U.S. transit agencies. The significance of lift failures can be appreciated from the experience reported by the New York City Transit (NYCT) Department of Buses. The NYCT reported over a 19 percent increase in passengers using wheelchairs boarding from October 1996 to October 1997. For October 1997, the number of wheelchair boardings was 42,641 (Reference 19). The NYCT reported that lift failures were their most frequent causes of road calls, and represented about 12 percent of all road calls in 1997 (Reference 20). The system-wide mean distance between road calls due to lift failures was reported to be 19,101 miles for 1997.

In the study, "An Evaluation of Accessible Transit Buses in Vancouver and Victoria," a comprehensive evaluation was made between low-floor ramp equipped buses in Victoria and high-floor lift equipped buses in Vancouver (Reference 10). One of the findings of the study was that the cost of maintaining lifts was significantly higher ($1,500 per year per bus) than the cost of maintaining ramps ($50 per year per bus).

A recent study on "Evaluating Transit Operations for Individuals with Disabilities," reported a clear savings in maintenance cost between ramp maintenance at the AATA and lift maintenance at the MTD, with no measurable difference in other maintenance costs. The annual maintenance cost for ramps was $300 compared to an annual maintenance cost for lifts of $2,400 (Reference 4).

2.6.1.2 Experiences with Radial Tires. All of the low-floor buses at the transit agencies that were interviewed used a low-profile radial tire, either a 275/70R 22.5 or a 305/70R 22.5. Two bus manufacturers (Gillig Corporation and North American Bus Industries) have a standard transit tire as an option. All of the experience at the time this report was written has been with low profile radial tires. The loaded radius of a low-profile tire is less than that of the standard tire resulting in more revolutions per mile as can be seen in Table 2.15. Since more revolutions are required to travel the same distance, it is reasonable to anticipate tire life to be proportional to the difference in the number of rotations.

All transit agencies indicated that the low profile tire was providing from 20 to 30 percent less life. The AATA reported the average life for their low profile tires was 56,228 miles. The VRTS reported an average life of 71,961 miles for new low profile tires, and an average of 31,639 miles for retread low profile tires. The retread tires are only used on the rear axle. The MTD said that their low profile tire life averaged about 50,000 miles, and the PTS was obtaining an average life of about 43,900 miles.

Other transit agencies reported their tire experience as a percentage compared to their experience with the standard tires used on their high-floor buses. The CTA said that they were experiencing about 20 percent shorter life with the low profile tire. The MARTA said that they were not seeing any significant change in fleet tire costs since the introduction of low-floor buses with low profile tires in their fleet. The CDTA has a lease agreement for their tires. For the first year of low-floor bus operations, the lease cost was about 35 percent higher for the low profile tires. Under a new 5-year lease agreement, the lease cost differential is significantly lower, about 19 percent more for the low profile tires during the first year of the new lease, and declining to about 12 percent more for the fifth year of the lease. The CDTA low-floor buses use the 305/70R 22.5 tire.

Other experiences that were reported by transit agencies were more abrasion of the side walls of the low profile radial tires and wheel damage. The dimensions of the low profile tire are such that the wheel rims are more likely to be damaged by hitting curbs than with a standard size tire. The MCTS changed from 275/70R 22.5 tires to 305/70R 22.5 tires to reduce the wheel rim damage from curb hits. The MCTS reported that the change in tires had corrected the problem.

The STCUM said that it was too early to evaluate their experiences of tire life. However, they did report to have observed a higher wear rate on the curb-side dual tires compared to the street-side dual tires (3/32 wear on street side tires to 7/32 wear on the curb side tires). The wear rate difference was thought to have been caused by the right side tires slipping. During tests of the bus at the Altoona Bus Testing Center, a weight difference between the right and left dual tires of 2,200 pounds was measured (Reference 16).

**Table 2.15 Comparison of Low-Profile
and Standard Transit Tires**

Tire Size	Revolutions Per Mile (RPM)	Increase of Revolutions Low Profile Versus Standard
Standard Tire 12R 22.5	483	- - -
275/70R 22.5	544	12.6%
305/70R 22.5	525	8.7%

Source: Information from Tire Manufacturers

2.6.1.3 Experiences with Brakes on Low-Floor Buses. The changes in the brake systems of a low-floor bus from a brake system of a high-floor bus are the location of components and different routing of the tubing. The functional design of the brake system is essentially the same, and the foundation brakes are the same size. Therefore, one would expect the performance of the brake system in the low-floor buses to be similar to that obtained on the high-floor buses. However, the experience has been different. The problems discussed in the following paragraphs <u>appear to have resulted from new bus design rather than low-floor bus design</u>.

Initially with the CTA low-floor buses, there were problems with the brake effort balance between front and rear brakes, the timing of brake application, and the short life of the brake linings. The bus manufacturer conducted field tests at the CTA to determine the causes of the problems. A field retrofit program (consisting of rerouting of the brake airline and changes in the valving) was then conducted to correct the imbalance and timing problems. The bus manufacturer indicated that it was important that proper cutting of the brake block to match the drum be done to obtain satisfactory lining life and brake performance.

The CTA reported that initially they were experiencing 16,000 to 18,000 miles between rear brake relines, but now they are obtaining 35,000 to 40,000 miles between rear brake relines. The CTA rear brake reline interval goal is 60,000 miles, and it is expected to be reached. Other brake system changes at the CTA included changing the control of the retarder (from a brake pedal only control to a combination of both brake and accelerator control) and the removal of the heat shields on the rear brakes.

The MTD reported obtaining 37,000 to 41,000 miles between relines for the rear brakes of their low-floor buses, and over 100,000 miles for the front brakes. The MTD controls the retarder by the accelerator pedal only to obtain the maximum braking effort from the retarder. The reline interval for the rear brakes of their comparable high-floor buses was over 50,000 miles, which is about a 20 percent longer interval. However, the reline interval for the high-floor front brakes was about 45,000 miles compared to a front brake reline interval of over 100,000 miles for their low-floor buses.

The VRTS reported an average rear brake reline interval of over 46,500 miles for their low-floor buses, and an average reline interval for the front brakes of over 133,000 miles. The retarder control is by the brake pedal at the VRTS.

The PTS reported longer brake life for their low-floor buses over their high-floor buses. The PTS brake reline intervals for their low-floor buses were approximately 50,000 miles for the rear brakes and 100,000 miles for the front brakes. In comparison, the reline intervals for their high-floor buses were 25,000 to 30,000 miles for the rear and about 40,000 miles for the front.

The low-floor buses at the CDTA, the STCUM, and the STRSM have only been in operation a short time. The STCUM and the STRSM did not have sufficient mileage on their low-floor buses to have experienced enough brake relines to report on any differences in brake life between their high-floor and low-floor buses. The early experience at CDTA indicates about 20,000 less miles for the reline intervals of their low-floor buses compared to their high-floor buses.

The CT found that the initial drum to lining contact was one of the primary factors affecting performance and life of brakes on their buses (including low-floor). Drum to lining contact is sensitive to cam size and tolerances and to machining practices. Factors unique to low-floor buses were proper balancing of the brake effort to both axles, and the correct supply of shoes and linings.

2.6.2 *Maintenance Facilities Impacts*

The changes needed in the maintenance facilities with the addition of low-floor buses to a fleet have been minimal. All of the transit agencies interviewed were using a combination of hoists and pits for the inspections, preventive maintenance, and repair of their low-floor buses. In the case of hoists, several transit agencies had fabricated simple fixtures to adapt their existing hoists to the undercarriage of their low-floor buses. No changes had been made to the pits. With the low-floor bus, the mechanic has less head room because the low-floor bus does not have the 12 to 15 inches of space under the floor that the high-floor buses have. However, because most, if not all, of the components that were located under the floor of a high-floor bus are now located in the roof or engine compartment areas, there is less need for a mechanic to work under the low-floor bus.

To reach the components now located in the roof area, some transit agencies use step ladders, while other have movable work platforms. The CTA has a powered scissors platform that they use at their North Park Garage. A photo of the platform is shown in Figure 2.7.

All transit agencies have purchased some special tools and adaptors that were needed for repair and maintenance of their new low-floor buses. In part, these new tools and adaptors were required because their low-floor buses used axles, brakes, suspensions, and transmissions that were not used in their current fleets. These additional

Figure 2.7 A Powered Work Platform for Maintenance of Components Located in the Roof Area

Figure 2.8 The Bus Washer at CTA North Park Garage

2.7 Safety Experiences

tools and fixtures are more a result of a change in bus rather than because the bus was low-floor.

Several of the transit agencies said that they had made some adjustments of the brushes in the bus washing system. These adjustments were necessary because the side skirts of a low-floor bus are 4 to 6 inches lower than those on a high-floor bus. The CTA fabricated a shim for their tire guide in the bus washer at their North Park Garage. A photo of the shim is shown in Figure 2.8. The shim was fabricated so that the low-floor bus wheel would not contact the curb as the bus travels through the washer.

When asked about the safety experiences with their low-floor buses, all transit agencies were satisfied with their experiences to date. However, none had available reports or data that would directly support their perceptions, such as a comparison of low-floor bus safety incidents with high-floor bus safety incidents on a comparable exposure basis. The low-floor buses were, in all cases, the newest bus in the fleets, and it was a general practice to maximize the use of the low-floor buses. As a result, the low-floor buses would accumulate more miles and hours per bus than other buses in the fleet. Also, there was a tendency to deploy the low-floor buses on the routes with high ridership. As a result of these practices, the exposure to passenger accidents of the low-floor buses was generally higher than the exposure of the high-floor buses.

An example of such a situation was found at the Phoenix Transit System (PTS). The PTS provided the accident data given in

Table 2.16. The PTS cautioned that the fact that the low-floor bus accidents are a little higher could be attributed to the fact that the low-floor buses are on routes having more exposure. The routes with low-floor buses are heavier and busier in terms of both vehicles on the road and passengers on board. The low-floor buses were also exposed to a higher frequency of trips than the high-floor buses.

Also, at the MCTS and the CT, the number of slips and falls incidents reported for their low-floor buses was higher than for their high-floor fleet; however, the safety staff again cautioned that direct comparisons would not be appropriate since the low-floor buses were being used more hours of the day, and were assigned routes with heavy ridership.

Typically, the available safety statistics that are recorded by transit agencies are by type and number of incidents along with factors such as: date, bus number, and operator identification. Some also include data on factors such as: location, driving conditions, time of day, route, and traffic conditions. The safety databases generally do not include data on factors such as: number of passengers transported by the bus, ambulatory capabilities of the passenger involved, vehicle hours or vehicle miles. Also, some transit agencies will not make their accident reports available to the public. As a result, a statistically valid safety comparison of low-floor buses versus high-floor buses in a fleet for passenger accidents, many times cannot be made from the available data.

The CDTA low-floor fleet is 21 buses, which is approximately nine percent of their total fleet of standard size buses. In 1997, the CDTA had a total of 30 boarding accidents with 8 (26 percent) occurring on the low-floor buses. The CDTA said that the higher than expected number might be attributed to the original kneeling sequence for their low-floor buses. Their buses would kneel after the door was fully open. Occasionally, passengers would try to board as the buses started to kneel, and sometimes they would fall. The kneeling sequence was modified during the Fall of 1997 to be simultaneous with the opening of the door, and only one boarding incident has occurred on their low-floor buses since the modification. The CDTA had 50 onboard incidents for 1997, and 7 (14 percent) were on their low-floor buses. Most of the incidents occurred in the front of the low-floor bus, between the farebox and the first row of seats. The CDTA experienced 65 alighting incidents during 1997, and only 3 (5 percent) occurred on the low-floor buses. The CDTA viewed this encouraging experience as hope for future reduction in alighting incidents.

The higher frequency of slips and falls in the interior of the low-floor buses also could be related to the lack of an adequate number of handholds in the front portion of a low-floor bus. The MTD said that people tend to lose their balance at the front of the bus because there are not enough handholds. The MTD, CT, and others have received complaints from seniors about the lack of handholds. In a recent report (Reference 13), it was recommended that a stanchion should always be within reach when a passenger is passing through the bus, so that the aisles can be negotiated when the bus is in motion. The report further points out that for low-floor buses with two wheelchair positions in the front, it is particularly difficult to provide an adequate number of stanchions and handrails in the front of the bus. Some transit agencies have

Table 2.16 High and Low-Floor Bus Accident Experience[*]

	Type of Accident			
	Passenger (Low-Floor)	Passenger (High-Floor)	Vehicle (Low-Floor)	Vehicle (High-Floor)
Accidents Per 100,000 Miles	.66	.55	2.45	1.99
Accidents	29	51	108	184

Source: Phoenix Transit System

---

[*] For the period of 10/1/96 through 9/30/97.

placed straps on the horizontal rails mounted from the ceiling to provide something for the customer to grasp. However, these straps are not reachable by some customers. The harsh braking of low-floor buses reported at some transit agencies may have also contributed to the number of slips and falls in the interior of the low-floor buses. It needs to be pointed out that no data that supports either of these conjectures were found during this study.

During the initial months of operation before the problems with the brake system had been resolved, some transit agencies reported incidences of sliding, skidding, and fish-tailing with their low-floor buses during slippery road conditions. These issues appear to be resolved with the changes made to the braking system. Although, the CTA did comment that their operators continue to complain that the "backend breaks out" with wet pavements. The CTA pointed out that the surfaces of their streets were quite smooth, and perhaps contributed to the problem. The CTA is conducting tests with the tire companies to evaluate different tread patterns. The operators can turn off the retarder when road conditions are slippery.

One safety issue that could be evaluated was the safety experiences related to the interior steps in the aisle leading to the rear of some of the low-floor buses. When asked whether or not any safety incidents had occurred because of the steps, all transit agencies that were operating low-floor buses with steps reported that they have not had any safety incident caused by the steps. The steps in the aisle have been perceived as a safety hazard by both transit customers and transit staff. Concerns about the steps were reported in previous studies (References 1 and 3), and in many of the customer surveys that were discussed earlier in the section on Customer Satisfaction and Acceptance (References 5, 6, 7, 9, and 11). However, the operating experiences to date do not indicate that the steps represent a safety hazard. There may be a bias involved in these experiences, since customers that have difficulty with steps or do not like steps are more likely to avoid using steps when possible.

2.8 Operator and Mechanic Acceptance and Satisfaction

2.8.1 *Operators*

At all of the transit agencies interviewed, the operators were satisfied with the low-floor buses. The most frequently mentioned comments from operators about what they liked were: the ease of boarding, the handling and quickness of the bus, the eye contact with the customers, and the ease of manual operation of the ramp. The most frequent operator comments about what they do not like about the bus were: lack of seats and room for standees and the steps in the aisle to the rear of the bus.

One of the most frequent comments operators make about how they feel about their low-floor buses is the eye level contact that they now have with customers as they board. Some add that it is helpful to be able to look down on some of their more lively school customers.

The MARTA and the NYCT conducted surveys of their operators on their opinions about the low-floor bus. The survey at MARTA was made about six months after placing the low-floor buses in revenue service. A low-floor demonstrator bus was operated by the NYCT for January to May 1997. Surveys were conducted of bus operators to learn their opinions about the bus. The findings of these surveys are given in the following paragraphs.

The MARTA operators were given a list of features on the low-floor buses, and asked to rate on a four point scale their evaluation. The results of the survey are listed below.

- "Visibility" was rated positively by over 95 percent of the respondents. Less than 4 percent gave it an unfavorable rating.
- "Noise Level" was given a positive rating by approximately 90 percent of the operators.
- "Handling" was liked by about 95 percent of the operators. The 5 percent that gave the bus a negative rating commented that "the lift on the low-floor buses scrapes the roads and the buses are often difficult to handle when turning."
- "Smoothness of Ride" was given a positive rating by about 89 percent of the operators. Comments from operators that gave negative ratings were: "some low-floor buses are slow accelerating" and "the buses ride rough, and scrape the road."
- "Interior Design" was given a positive rating by about 82 percent of the operators.
- "Passenger Safety When Using Rear Steps" was a concern of some operators, particularly when the bus was moving. About 70 percent of the operators thought that the steps were safe, but 30 percent gave this feature a negative rating.
- On "Overall Performance," about 94 percent gave the low-floor buses a positive rating.

During the demonstration of the low-floor bus at the NYCT, the operators that had driven the bus were asked six questions about features of the bus and what they thought of the bus overall. The responses of the NYCT operators are given below.

- The operators overwhelmingly like how the bus handled, the comfort of the Operator's seat, the view out of the bus, and the low-floor aspect.
- The largest concern of the operators was with the outside mirrors. They felt that the front right side mirror was too low, and posed a hazard to passengers. The left side mirror had a blind spot.
- Some of the operators were concerned about the two steps in the aisle and inadequate interior space for rush hour loads.

An operator with seventeen years of experience at Calgary Transit provided a written list of operator comments and concerns about their low-floor bus. A summary of the main comments follows:

- "Exit Door" - There is a longer delay in the activation of the exit door after the bus has stopped than with other buses in their fleet, which has resulted in customer complaints to the operator to open the door.
- "Ride Quality" - A large number of operators complain of the jerky ride quality of the bus.
- "Flow of Passengers" - Because the front area (adjacent to the wheel wells) of the bus is open, passengers like to stop and hold conversations with others. This is particularly true with students who tend to gather there. This impedes the free movement of other passengers to the rear of the bus. Once gathered there, it is very difficult to get them to move back, especially when there is a full standing load. It is sometimes difficult to get passengers to climb the steps to the rear of the bus.
- "Brakes" - A number of operators feel that excessive force is needed to activate the brakes. When there is a need for a "panic brake," the bus is difficult to steer. The operators prefer the retarder to be activated by the accelerator rather than the brake pedal.
- "Heating" - Some operators feel that the heater does not provide enough heat in extreme cold weather.
- "Vibration" - Some operators complain about higher vibration with the four cylinder engine.
- "Front Door" - The width of the frame of the front door panels is too wide and creates a blind spot when trying to see to the right at intersections.

2.8.2 *Mechanics*

The majority of the transit agencies reported that their mechanics were satisfied with their low-floor buses. There are some concerns because of the changes of the low-floor buses at some agencies. For example, some did not like to work on the roof of the bus, but others found this not to be a problem. Some mechanics said that they preferred working on the low-floor buses with the components located in the roof area because everything was cleaner.

A MARTA maintenance supervisor said that the maintenance accessibility is a little less on their low-floor buses, but not a serious problem. One item that had been a problem was access to make a valve adjustment on their diesel engines on their low-floor buses. An access panel from the inside of the bus was provided for their CNG low-floor buses, and the problem is considered solved.

The STCUM said that their mechanics had problems in accepting the new low-floor buses. The STCUM mechanics have had essentially one bus design for the last twenty years, so part of their concern was because of the many changes with the new bus, such as: location of components, tooling, procedures, and different engine, transmission, and axles.

The only comments received concerning the cleaning maintenance of the low-floor buses were related to the cleaning of the higher ceiling. Most agencies felt that there was no significant difference in the cleaning and servicing of a low-floor bus compared to a high-floor bus.

3.0 MARKET STATUS AND TRENDS

From 1991 to 1995, only two bus manufacturers were delivering heavy-duty, standard-size, low-floor buses to the North American market. During that time, over 96 percent of low-floor buses delivered were from one manufacturer. In 1996 and 1997, two more bus manufacturers began to deliver low-floor buses, and by 1998 two more bus manufacturers will be delivering low-floor buses. As of December 1997, the total number of standard and large-size low-floor buses delivered by all bus manufacturers was reported as 2,812, and another 2,657 were on order. A breakdown by manufacturer is given in Table 3.1.

The growth of the low-floor bus market has increased rapidly in the last two years with the entry of all manufacturers of heavy-duty buses into the market. Table 3.2 and Figure 3.1 show the growth by year of the low-floor bus market.

At the end of 1996, the size of the national heavy-duty bus (35- to 60-foot) fleets in the U.S. and Canada were 50,344 and 10,391 respectively (References 29 and 30). Assuming buses are replaced after 15 years of service in the U.S., and after 18 years of service in Canada, the annual markets for these types of buses should be about 3,350 for the U.S., and 570 for Canada. However, historically the markets have been smaller than this: averaging only 3,290 buses per year for the combined markets. Table 3.3 gives the number of buses purchased in the U.S. and Canada for the years of 1991 to 1996.

The low-floor bus purchases in 1997 are estimated to be between 30 to 40 percent of all heavy-duty buses purchased by transit agencies in North America. In response to a

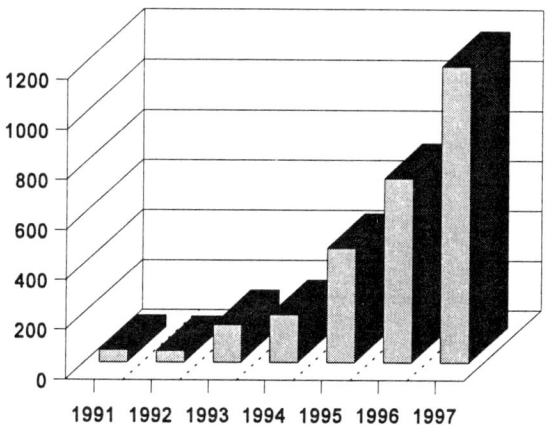

Figure 3.1 Growth in the Delivery of Low-Floor Buses[a]

Source: Bus Manufacturers

---

[a] Includes 35, 40, and 60-foot buses.

survey question, three of the bus manufacturers projected that by the year 2000 that 50 to 90 percent of their sales would be low-floor models.

In 1997, APTA Transit Vehicle Data Book reports the orders of buses, as of January 1997, for all sizes of buses not including those used in a demand responsive mode as 5,144. The data were collected from one hundred one transit agencies, including all of the largest thirty agencies in the U.S. The APTA Vehicle Data Book also stated that 1,044 of these orders were for buses equipped with ramps. This would mean that slightly over 20 percent of all orders are for low-floor buses.

Table 3.1 Low-Floor Bus Market Status[a]

Bus Manufacturer	Delivered	On Order[b]
Gillig Corporation		543
Neoplan USA Corporation	32	0
New Flyer Industries Limited	2,303	424
North American Bus Industries		608
Nova Bus Corporation	406	592
Orion Bus Industries	71	490
Totals	2,812	2,657

Source: Bus Manufacturers

---

[a] Includes 35, 40, and 60-foot buses, through 1997.
[b] Includes all options.

Table 3.2 Low-Floor Buses Delivered During 1991 to 1997[a]

Year	NEO	NFIL	NOV	OBI	Totals
1991		48			48
1992	2	42			44
1993	10	139			149
1994	12	178			190
1995	8	450			458
1996		696	30	12	738
1997		750	376	59	1,185
Totals	32	2,303	406	71	2,812

Source: Bus Manufacturers

---

[a] Includes 35, 40, and 60-foot buses.

Table 3.3 Number of Heavy-Duty Transit Buses Purchased by Year

Year	United States[a]	Canada[b]	Totals
1991	2,897	528	3,425
1992	2,120	549	2,669
1993	2,909	163	3,072
1994	2,938	250	3,188
1995	3,166	341	3,507
1996	3,396	486	3,882
Totals	17,426	2,317	19,743
Average Per Year	2,904	386	3,290

Sources: References 26 and 27

---

[a] Includes buses of 32.5 to 60-foot in length.
[b] Includes 35, 40 and 60-foot buses.

4.0 TECHNOLOGY STATUS AND DEVELOPMENTS

4.1 Status of Bus Manufacturers

Currently, there are six manufacturers in North America that are offering heavy-duty, low-floor buses to the transit market. Some of the technical characteristics of the 40-foot, low-floor models by manufacturer are given in Table 4.1. The sizes of low-floor buses that are currently offered or are under development for each manufacturer are identified in Table 4.2. As can be seen in Table 4.2, all manufacturers have a 40-foot model, and four have (or plan to have) a 35-foot model. The various propulsion and fuel options that are available from each manufacturer are identified in Tables 4.3 and 4.4.

4.2 Developments in Technology

There are several projects that could lead to significant advances in body and propulsion technologies that are applicable to future low-floor bus developments. The Advance Technology Transit Bus (ATTB) program was initiated in 1992 with the objective of developing a lightweight, low-floor, low-emission transit bus. There are two programs to develop a fuel cell powered bus, one of which is integrated in a low-floor bus. There are several hybrid electric propulsion system projects that are expected to reach the production stage in the near future. Each of these programs is discussed in the following sections. The last two subsections on developments in technology discuss new approaches under development in Europe. The first discusses innovative approaches to wheelchair securement involving "rear facing protected position" designs that are being adopted in Europe. The last subsection discusses level boarding with low-floor buses, and some of the experiences with level boarding in Europe.

4.2.1 Advanced Technology Transit Bus

The ATTB is a major Federal project to develop a 40-foot transit bus that meets Federal requirements for axle loads, emissions, and accessibility, a maximum unit price of $300,000 (1992 dollars), low operating costs, and can accommodate 43 seated and 29 standee passengers. A layout of an example seating arrangement is given in Figure 4.1.

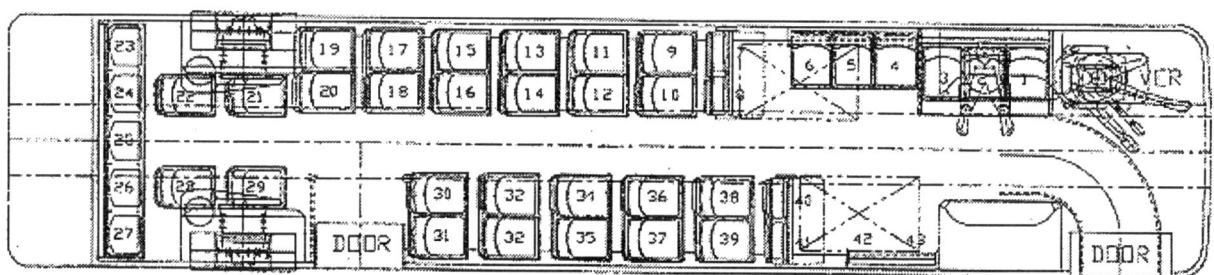

Figure 4.1 Example Seating Layout for the ATTB

Source: Reference 34

Table 4.1 Technical Characteristics of 40-Foot, Low-Floor Buses

Characteristic	Gillig	Neoplan USA	New Flyer Industries	North American Bus Industries	Nova Bus	Orion Bus Industries
Model Identification	Low-Floor Bus	AN440L	D40L	40LFW	LFS	Orion VI
Height, Inches	114.5	115.5[a]	111	114	123[a]	118.5[b]
Wheelbase, Inches	284	274	293	276	244	278
Turning Radius, Feet	42.5	42	44.1	44	41.5	39.6
Approach Angle, Degrees	9	10	9.2	9	9	10
Departure Angle, Degrees	10	9	9.3	9	9	9
Breakover Angle, Degrees	10	10	8.3	10	9.5	10
1st Door Entr. Ht. (Not Kneeled), Inches	12.5[c]	14	14.5	14 – 15[d]	14.6	14.5
2nd Door Exit Ht. (Not Kneeled), Inches	13.75[c]	15	14.5	14 – 15[d]	14.6	14.5[e]
Kneeling Capacity: Front Door (in Inches) Rear Door	3 3	3 1	3 3	3 3+	5 5	3.5 3.5
Ramp Location, Front/Rear Door	F	Both	Both	Both	Both	F
Wheelchair Location, Front/Rear	F	Both	Both	Both	Both	F
Maximum Number of Seats	40	42[f]	39	37	39[f]	35
Maximum Capacity, (GVWR - CW) / 150	87	77	82	77	82	91
GVWR, Pounds	37,920	37,920	39,190	40,600	39,550	41,750
Curb Weight, Pounds	24,800	26,325	26,750	29,000	27,200	28,000

Source: Bus Manufacturers

(a) With roof mounted air conditioning unit.
(b) Over access hatch.
(c) Entrance height with standard profile tires is 15 inches, and the exit height is 16.25 inches.
(d) Entrance and exit heights will depend on the tires used.
(e) Height of exit behind the rear axle is 14.5 inches.
(f) With four rear-facing seats.

Table 4.2 Size of Heavy-Duty, Low-Floor Buses Offered by Manufacturers

Manufacturer	Size of Buses				
	30-Foot	35-Foot	40-Foot	45-Foot	Artics
Gillig Corporation		X	X		
Neoplan USA Corporation		X	X	X	
New Flyer Industries Limited	X	X	X		X
North American Bus Industries		X[a]	X		
Nova Bus Corporation			X		
Orion Bus Industries			X		

Source: Bus Manufacturers

[a] The 35-foot model is under development.

Table 4.3 Propulsion Options Offered by Manufacturers

Manufacturer	Propulsion Option		
	HYB-Elec	Fuel Cell	Trolley
Gillig Corporation	X[a]		
Neoplan USA Corporation			
New Flyer Industries Limited	X[a]	X	X
North American Bus Industries			
Nova Bus Corporation	X[a]	X[a]	
Orion Bus Industries	X		

Source: Bus Manufacturers

[a] Planned or under development.

Table 4.4 Fuel Options Offered by Manufacturers

Manufacturer	Fuel Option		
	Diesel	CNG[a]	LNG[b]
Gillig Corporation	X		
Neoplan USA Corporation	X		
New Flyer Industries Limited	X	X	X
North American Bus Industries	X	X	X
Nova Bus Corporation	X	X	
Orion Bus Industries	X	X	

Source: Bus Manufacturers

[a] Compressed natural gas.
[b] Liquefied natural gas.

The ATTB environmental design goals are the California Air Resources Board (CARB) Low Emission Vehicle (LEV) requirements for urban buses. The program calls for the design and fabrication of six prototypes. Field testing is scheduled through 1998. The physical characteristics of the ATTB are given in Table 4.5.

The first bus is an engineering test bed that is being used to evaluate various subsystems and to validate the design approach. The second bus incorporated design improvements developed with the first unit, and is the durability test bed. Bus number 2 is currently being tested at the Altoona Bus Testing Center. The remaining three units will be used for demonstrations and revenue service tests at several cities throughout the U.S.

4.2.2 Fuel Cell Developments

There are two efforts underway to power a transit bus with fuel cell technology. One is the Federal Transit Administration (FTA) Fuel Cell Transit Bus Program, and the other is the Ballard Fuel Cell which has been integrated in an NFIL D40L bus. While the test bed used in the FTA program is a high-floor bus, if successful the technology could be used in a low-floor bus. The incentives for considering fuel cell technology are a pollution free bus service, use of a non-fossil fuel, and an increase in range over battery technologies.

The FTA program is a joint program with the Department of Energy (DOE), and is managed by the Georgetown University. The program objective is to integrate a phosphoric acid fuel cell in a 40-foot transit bus (RTS). Methanol is fed to a reformer which produces the hydrogen gas used by the phosphoric acid fuel cell to produce electric energy. A prototype is to be delivered in the Summer of 1998 for tests and evaluation.

Ballard Power Systems has installed fuel cell engines in seven NFIL D40L buses. Three of these buses have been sold to the CTA and three to BC Transit Vancouver. The buses were delivered in 1997. The Ballard fuel cell uses hydrogen gas stored in high pressure cylinders, similar to those used for CNG storage. The hydrogen gas is fed into a Proton Exchange Membrane (PEM) fuel cell which through an electrochemical process produces electric power and water vapor. The CTA fuel cell buses will be placed in revenue service by March 1998 on three routes that travel through the downtown area for test and evaluation of the technology.

4.2.3 Hybrid Electric Developments

There are several programs underway to develop a hybrid electric propulsion system for transit buses. One program that will have buses placed in revenue service in the near future is the Orion VI Low-Floor Hybrid-Electric bus. The New Jersey Transit has ordered four buses and they will be delivered in the first quarter of 1998. The NYCT has ten buses on order, and they are scheduled to be delivered in the second quarter of 1998. The bus uses a Lockheed Martin hybrid electric propulsion involving a DDC Series 30 engine, a 110kW generator, and AC traction motor, an advanced lead acid battery pack, and an electric power control system.

The Gillig Corporation is developing a hybrid electric propulsion system for their

Table 4.5 Technical Characteristics of the ATTB

Characteristics	
Length, feet	40
Height, inches	118.4
Wheelbase, inches	301
Turning Radius, feet	42.5
Approach Angle, degrees	10
Departure Angle, degrees	10
1st Door Entrance Height (not kneeled), inches	14
2nd Door Entrance Height (not kneeled), inches	14
Kneeling Capability (in inches) Front Rear	3
Ramp Location, Front/Rear Door	F
Wheelchair Location, Front/Rear	F
Maximum Number of Seats	43
Maximum Capacity, (GVWR - CW)/150	77
Gross Vehicle Weight Rating (GVWR), pounds	31,960
Curb Weight, pounds	20,355
Engine	DDC Series 30 G
Generator	EEMCO AC Induction (200kw)
Wheel Motor	Unique Mobility DC Perm. Mag.
Front Tire	SR275/70R22.5
Rear Tire	SR385/65R22.5

Source: References 34 and 35

buses. The first propulsion system will be tested in a Phantom 40-foot bus that will be delivered to Golden Gate later this year. The Gillig hybrid-electric propulsion system is similar in approach to the Lockheed Martin system, and includes an engine, generator, traction motor, battery pack, and power controller. Gillig plans to use the technology in their low-floor bus, and be in production in 3 to 5 years.

The FTA DUETS program involves the development of an advanced hybrid electric propulsion system for buses. The Nova Bus Corporation is the contractor for the program. The test bed vehicle is an RTS bus that has two small rotary natural gas engines coupled to a generator. Power from the generator flows to the power control unit then to two wheel hub motors. The propulsion system also includes a lead acid battery storage system. A demonstration test of the system is scheduled to begin in 1998.

4.2.4 Protected Position Design for Wheelchair Accommodation

European research and standards development efforts (References 12 and 31) have focused on an innovative approach to accommodating passengers in wheelchairs on low-floor buses, involving a "protected position" on the vehicle. This concept involves two major elements: 1) a clear rectangular floor area of approximately 55 by 28 inches, where a person in a wheelchair can position themselves in a rear-facing position, and 2) a load bearing back and head rest, which protects the passenger in case of rapid deceleration. Flip-up seats are usually provided to be used by other passengers when no passenger in a wheelchair is present. In addition, a vertical aisle stanchion is typically provided to prevent the wheelchair sliding into the aisle during bus turning movements.

Such an approach is reported to provide: the same level of safety afforded to other seated bus passengers; more independence of the passenger in the wheelchair during boarding, riding, and alighting; and a safe wheelchair location without the use of hooks or belts. Further, the approach does not require the assistance of the operator. However, the wheelchair passenger must face to the rear, which is not an issue in Europe, but is more of an issue for North American buses. However, rear-facing seats are common in trains and subways in North America.

This approach appears to offer many advantages and a high level of safety. It has become the widely accepted standard in Europe, and the Canadian Urban Transit Association has been exploring its transferability to Canadian transit systems (Reference 32). As a result, several Canadian transit systems have adopted this approach. Examples of the "protected position" can be seen in Figures 2.5 and 4.2. The "protected position" does not meet the ADA requirement of a 20g deceleration, but studies have shown that even extreme braking on buses rarely exceed 0.5g (References 31 and 33). A waiver would be required to use the "protected position" approach in the United States.

4.2.5 Level Boarding Developments

According to a recent European Community (EC) report (Reference 15), the introduction of low-floor buses should be seen as one step along the path to a more

Figure 4.2 Hamilton Street Railway Low-Floor Bus with Protected Position

Source: Canadian Urban Transit Association

passenger friendly transport system. The next steps that are being proposed are level boarding, improvements in passenger information, and improvements in bus stop facilities. Level access for all customers is regarded as one of the most important features of an attractive and modern means of public transport.

In several cities in France and Germany, level board tests are underway. Level boarding is accomplished by raising the level of the bus stop platform to the level of the low-floor bus entrance. To minimize the horizontal gap between the bus entrance and the bus stop platform, the bus must be consistently brought close to the curb. It is difficult for operators to consistently steer the bus close to the curb without damaging the tire or bus body. In several cities in Germany they are experimenting with special curb stones that are claimed to assist the operators in steering the bus to the curb without damaging the tires. A photo of a "Bus Kap" in Aachen, Germany using this approach is shown in Figure 4.3. In this case, the bus stop was brought out to the traffic lane, and the bus would stop in the traffic lane. Since the honor fare collection system enables all doors to be used to board and alight, and there is no time lost by the bus trying to re-enter the traffic stream, the dwell time is quite short. Another approach used in Caen, France is shown in Figure 4.4. In this case, a steel tube imbedded in the curb is used to protect the tire. In Grenoble, France, experiments are underway to use optical guidance to steer the bus to the stop. In Essen, Germany, a guided bus route uses the median of a four lane highway to Kray. There are three stations located along the route. The route has only low-floor buses operating on the route. The guided bus system operates in this case like a rubber tired rail system. The station platforms are at the same level as the floor level of the guided bus. The interface between vehicle and station platform is as good as any high platform rail system. A photo of a low-floor guided bus stopped at a station is shown in Figure 4.5.

In August 1997, a successful demonstration of full automatic control of two MTA low-floor buses was accomplished. The buses were equipped with both vision and radar sensors to control the bus in both lateral and longitudinal directions. Such technology could also be used to steer a bus close to a bus stop platform.

Figure 4.3 Raised Bus Stop in Aachen, Germany

Figure 4.4 Raised Bus Stop in Caen, France

Figure 4.5 Low-Floor Guided Bus at a Station in Essen

5.0 CONCLUSIONS AND RECOMMENDATIONS

Since their first deployment in 1991, low-floor buses have increasingly become the choice of transit agencies in both the United States and Canada. By December 1997, there were over 2,800 low-floor buses in operation and over 2,600 on order in North America. There are six manufacturers that are offering heavy-duty, standard-size, low-floor buses to the transit market.

5.1 Conclusions

The significant findings from interviews with transit agencies operating low-floor buses and discussions with bus manufacturers are provided below:

5.1.1 Customer Satisfaction and Acceptance

- Customers liked the ease of boarding and alighting of the low-floor buses. Seniors and people with disabilities expressed even a stronger preference for low-floor buses. Most wheelchair passengers preferred a ramp over a lift.
- Other features that customers liked were the ability to see out of the larger windows, the feeling of a spacious environment with the higher ceilings, and places to put packages.
- Customers also had complaints concerning issues such as: lack of seats, crowding, noise and vibration, windows fogged ("can't see out"), concerns about the safety of the steps in the aisle, and a "jerky" ride. Only one transit agency had received many vocal customer complaints about their low-floor buses. The main focus of their complaints was crowding and inability to move freely through the bus, although it should be noted that the average loads of the buses were much higher at this transit agency.
- Six transit agencies had conducted customer surveys. A large majority of customers gave a positive rating of the low-floor bus, and only four to nine percent gave a negative rating for their low-floor bus. One survey found that peak period riders preferred the conventional high-floor bus because the low-floor buses had less seats and lack of room for standees, while the non-peak riders preferred the low-floor bus.

5.1.2 Customer Comfort and Environment

- Overall, the customers were satisfied with the comfort and environment of the low-floor buses.
- Some complaints had also been received:

- During rainy or snowy days, the windows can become obscured with road grime and spray, making it difficult to see out.
- On very cold days, passengers' feet got cold, and some customers were bothered by the noise and/or vibration of the low-floor bus.
- Sudden and unexpected changes in acceleration and deceleration arising from harsh braking or lack of smooth transition in power gave a jerky ride.

The initial low-floor buses had inadequate heating systems. Improvements made in the heating systems are improving the situation, except perhaps for very cold climates. The vibration complaints were usually received with buses powered by four cylinder engines. The noise complaints usually came from passengers seated in the rear of the bus next to the engine compartment.

- Tests conducted by CUTA found that only one of the low-floor buses tested met an ASHRAE Standard for fresh air in the passenger compartment. The test also indicated problems with uneven heat distribution in the passenger compartment.
- Several of the transit agencies reported having dusty buses. The reasons for the higher level of dust intrusion are not fully understood.

5.1.3 Capacity and Ridership

- For the currently available low-floor, 40-foot buses, the maximum number of seats (using only front and aisle-facing) range from 35 to 40, compared with a range of 43 to 45 for high-floor models. If a transit agency's loading standard is to provide a seat for all expected customers, then the loss in capacity on a route would be proportional to the reduction in the number of seats, assuming no changes in schedule speed and headway.
- Most agencies interviewed reported that they had made no changes in their schedules or added buses with the introduction of low-floor buses in their system. Two agencies reported that the lower capacity of their low-floor buses would probably require adding more buses on routes to maintain their service standards. They were experiencing rapid growth in ridership, and buses had been added to routes. They could not say what portion of the need for more buses was due to increase in riders or what portion was caused by the lower capacity of their low-floor buses.
- None of the agencies operated routes with all low-floor buses during the peak periods.
- The CTA reported no changes were required when they introduced the low-floor buses in their system. The CTA uses the same maximum capacity (70) for

their low-floor buses as is used for their high-floor buses when assigning buses to routes.
- The STCUM said that for scheduling purposes their low-floor bus with 39 seats had a "natural" capacity of 65 passengers, compared to a "natural" capacity of 80 for their high-floor buses. However, the STCUM is evaluating a new interior design for their low-floor buses which they feel has a "natural" capacity of 80, which is the same as their high-floor buses. While the new interior design provides an equivalent vehicle <u>capacity</u>, there are 24 percent fewer seats (31 versus 41), and the service <u>quality</u> (measured by the number of seats provided) would be lower.
- Boarding times for an ambulatory passenger on a low-floor bus were reported to be from 0.2 to 0.7 of a second faster. Alighting times for an ambulatory passenger were reported to be from 0.3 to 2.7 seconds faster, and, in one case, 0.3 second slower. The case of the slower alighting time was attributed to a change in how the exit door was activated.
- None of the agencies reported any increases in schedule speed with the introduction of low-floor buses to their fleet though little formal evaluation had been conducted.
- During the Paralympics, the boarding times for athletes in wheelchairs for both low-floor and high-floor buses were measured. The mean boarding times (not including maneuvering inside the bus or securement) for a low-floor bus was about 27.4 seconds, while the mean boarding time for a high-floor bus was about 46.4 seconds. The report also noted that only one deployment of a ramp is required, irrespective of the number of boarding or alighting persons with mobility aids.

5.1.4 *Vehicle Operating Experiences*

- All agencies were generally satisfied with the road clearance capabilities of the low-floor buses. Some reported that the protective skid for the ramp cam mechanism would occasionally ground on steep ramps, and some reported grounding on some high railroad crossings and large speed bumps.
- The low-floor buses tended to be quicker and had good handling characteristics.
- The CDTA reported some steering problems during a heavy, wet snow storm with their low-floor buses. Slush and ice became packed around the steering linkages, and restricted the operator's ability to steer the bus. The manufacturer has provided a fix that seems to be working.

5.1.5 Impacts on Maintenance

- Transit agencies were generally satisfied with their maintenance experiences. Many of the early problems experienced by the transit agencies <u>appear to be "new bus model" problems, rather than problems intrinsically related to a low-floor bus design</u>. All agencies had a "punch list" of problems that needed to be resolved.
- Three maintenance items that were consistently reported by the transit agencies as being significantly different in comparison with their high-floor buses were:

    - The operating experiences with the ramp have been universally positive. The U.S. transit agencies reported that service interruptions because of ramp failures either did not occur or were rare. Lift failure is a major cause of road calls for many U.S. transit agencies. In addition, the cost of maintaining lifts has been reported to be significantly higher than the cost of maintaining ramps. The costs per bus per year ranged from $50 to $300 for ramps and from $1,500 to $2,400 for lifts.
    - All of the low-floor buses at the transit agencies used a low-profile radial tire, either a 275/70R22.5 or a 305/70R22.5. All indicated that they were getting from 20 to 30 percent less miles with their low profile tires. Also, several agencies reported more wheel damage from hitting curbs with their low-floor buses. The STCUM has noted a higher wear rate on their curb side, dual tires compared with the street side, dual tires. The wear rate difference was thought to have been caused by the right side, dual tires slipping.
    - Problems reported with the brakes were: brake effort balance between front and rear brakes, timing of brake application, and the short life of brake linings. The bus manufacturer conducted a retrofit program and corrected the imbalance and timing problems. The life of brake linings is improving, but for many properties, it is still shorter than desired. The problems with the brakes appear to have resulted because the bus was a new bus design rather than a low-floor design.

5.1.6 Maintenance Facilities Impacts

- The changes needed in the maintenance facilities with the addition of low-floor buses to a fleet have been minimal. No changes had been made to the

maintenance pits. Some have fabricated fixtures to adapt their existing hoists to the undercarriage of their low-floor buses.
- To work on roof mounted components, some used step ladders; others used movable work platforms.
- All agencies have purchased some special tooling and adapters largely because it was a new bus in their fleet.
- Several agencies had made adjustments to the height of the brushes on their bus washer. The CTA had fabricated a shim for the tire guide of their bus washer so that the low-floor bus wheel would not contact the curb as it travels through the washer.

5.1.7 Safety Experiences

- All transit agencies were satisfied with their safety experiences with their low-floor buses. However, few had data to support their perceptions.
- Some transit agencies reported that the number of passenger accidents per low-floor bus was higher than the passenger accidents per bus for their high-floor fleet. <u>All</u> of the agencies <u>cautioned against</u> making a simple comparison of the data because of the small amount of data, and the exposure of the low-floor buses (more passengers and more miles per bus) tended to be higher than for their high-floor buses.
- Some agencies felt that the higher frequency of slips and falls of passengers occurring in the front of the low-floor buses could be related to the lack of an adequate number of handholds from the farebox to the first row of seats.
- The steps in the aisle have been perceived as a safety hazard by both transit customers and transit staff, and concerns about the steps were reported in several of the customer surveys. The operating experiences to date do not indicate that the steps represent a safety hazard. All transit agencies that were operating low-floor buses with steps in the aisle reported that they have not had any safety incidents caused by the steps.

5.1.8 Operator and Mechanic Acceptance and Satisfaction

- Overall, operators were satisfied with their low-floor buses. Operators liked the ease of customer boarding, the ease of using the ramp (and the ease of manual operation of the ramp), the quickness and handling of the bus, the improved visibility, and the eye level contact they have with customers. When asked about concerns, a senior operator at CT listed the following: congestion in the front of the bus, the flow of passengers to the rear

of the bus, insufficient heat during extremely cold weather, the jerky ride quality, and a blind spot created by the frame of the front door panels.
- Surveys conducted at MARTA and NYCT found that their operators liked the improved visibility, handling, and noise level, but expressed concerns about steps in the aisle and the right side mirror being too low (hazard to passengers).
- The majority of mechanics were satisfied with their low-floor buses. Some mechanics preferred to work on the low-floor buses since everything was cleaner and accessible (many components moved from under the bus to the roof area), while others expressed some concerns about working from ladders and elevated platforms.
- One service person pointed out that the higher ceilings were a little more difficult to clean. However, most agencies felt that there were no significant differences in the cleaning and servicing of the low-floor buses.

5.1.9 Market Status and Trends

- Only Neoplan USA and New Flyer Industries were delivering heavy-duty, low-floor buses from 1991 through 1995. Nova Bus and Orion Bus Industries began delivering low-floor models in 1996 and 1997. Gillig and North American Bus Industries will begin delivery of heavy-duty, low-floor buses in the first quarter of 1998.
- At the end of 1997, bus manufacturers reported that 2,812 low-floor buses had been delivered, and that they had orders for another 2,660.
- With the entry of more manufacturers to the low-floor market, the number of deliveries has grown rapidly. There were 1,185 low-floor buses (35, 40, and 60-foot) delivered in 1997.
- It is estimated that low-floor models were 30 to 40 percent of the 1997 heavy-duty bus market in North America. Three of the manufacturers estimated that their sales of buses in 2000 would be 50 to 90 percent low-floor models.

5.1.10 Technology Status and Developments

- All six of the manufacturers offer a 40-foot bus to the transit market, and four offer 35-foot models. Only one manufacturer offers 30, 35, 40, and 60-foot models.
- All have low-floor models powered by diesel engines. Four offer the option of compressed natural gas (CNG), and two have options for liquefied natural gas (LNG).
- There are several R&D programs underway that could lead to significant advances in

technologies used in low-floor buses.
- The ATTB is a major FTA program to develop a light-weight, low emission, low operating cost, low-floor bus for the next century. Six prototypes have been fabricated. Testing is underway at the Altoona Bus Testing Center with one of the buses. Three of the prototypes will be demonstrated at various transit agencies during 1998.
- Ballard Power Systems has installed their fuel cell engine in seven New Flyer Industries low-floor buses. Three buses were delivered to both the CTA and the BC Transit-Vancouver for test and evaluation in revenue service.
- The FTA Fuel Cell Transit Bus Program is a cooperative program with the DOE to design a 40-foot bus powered by a fuel cell system. A prototype fuel cell system installed in a Nova Bus RTS will be delivered for demonstration and testing in the summer of 1998.
- A low-floor, hybrid-electric bus is under development by Orion Bus Industries and Lockheed Martin. The initial production models will be delivered to the New Jersey Transit (four buses) and the New York City Transit (ten buses) in the first half of 1998. These buses will be placed in revenue service for test and evaluation.
- The Gillig Corporation is developing a hybrid-electric propulsion system for their buses. The first delivery will be in a Phantom to be delivered to Golden Gate in the spring of 1998. A low-floor bus using this propulsion system is expected to be in production in 3 to 5 years.
- Most European and a number of Canadian transit systems are adopting the rear-facing "protected position" design to accommodate passengers in wheelchairs. This approach uses a backrest to protect the passenger during deceleration. It is extremely attractive because it involves no straps or mechanical devices, no operator involvement, and enhanced passenger independence.
- Several cities in Europe are demonstrating various approaches to level boarding with low-floor buses. To achieve an acceptable horizontal gap between the bus entrance and the station platform, some method of aiding the operator or automatically steering the bus close to the curb is required. Mechanical, optical, and electronic guidance approaches are under evaluation.

5.2 Recommendations

Based upon the insights gained during the course of this study, the following research topics are recommended for consideration:

- **Reduction in Dwell Times.** Low-floor buses enable the faster boarding and alighting of passengers. For ambulatory passengers, the average reported time savings was about 0.5 seconds per passenger, and for passengers with disabilities the average reported time savings was approximately 19 seconds. However, to take advantage of these quicker boarding and alighting times, a faster fare collection process is needed. For example, a "proof of payment" system or "smart card" system where bus passengers can use all doors would significantly shorten dwell times. Facilitating a fast and safe reentry of the bus into the traffic stream would aid in reducing dwell times. Buses in the province of Quebec, and more recently in the State of Washington, are given the right-of-way when they emerge from a bus stop to reenter the traffic stream. Bringing the bus stop adjacent to the traffic lane so that the bus stops in the traffic lane is another approach that has been implemented by some transit agencies.
- **Development of Level Boarding System.** Low-floor buses hold the potential to offer level boarding to bus customers comparable to those that exist for high platform rail systems. Various schemes are being tested in Europe to assist the operator to steer close to the curb of a raised bus stop platform. Automatic guidance approaches are also under development and evaluation. Mechanical guidance has been in use in Germany for over 15 years. Optical and electronic methods are also under development and evaluation. The development of a level boarding system for buses would benefit all customers and would aid in reducing dwell times, thus having beneficial effects on traffic flow and environmental pollution.
- **Improved Passenger Handholds in the Front of the Bus.** A high percentage of passenger slips and falls have occurred in the area between the farebox and the first row of seats. When the wheelchair positions are located in the front of the bus, there are distances of six to eight feet where vertical stanchions are not available for passengers to grasp as they move to the rear of the bus. The horizontal grab bar is too high for some passengers to reach. The straps used by some agencies have helped, but are not a complete solution. The straps do not provide a firm hand hold for the elderly, and some passengers cannot raise their arms to reach the strap. Improvements in passenger

handholds would reduce the passenger slips and falls while on the bus. This might, for example, build on the prototype efforts carried out at Calgary Transit.

REFERENCES

(1) King, R.D., "Low-Floor Buses," TCRP Synthesis 2, (1994).

(2) Schneider, W. And Beechbühl, A., "Defining the Low-Floor Bus: Its Advantages and Disadvantages," Paper presented at the International Union of Public Transport 49th International Congress, Stockholm (August 1991).

(3) Prentice, C. And Kershaw, D., "Low-Floor Bus Design Issues and Guidelines Study," Canadian Urban Transit Association, Report No. RD-94-3, (September 1994).

(4) "Evaluating Transit Operations for Individuals with Disabilities," Final Report (draft), TCRP Project B-1, Multisystems, Inc. & Crain & Associates, Inc., (April 1997).

(5) "Low-Floor Bus Survey," Calgary Transit, (December 1993).

(6) "Low-Floor and Standard Bus Surveys," Chicago Transit Authority, Technical Report SP93-04, (February 1993).

(7) "Low-Floor Bus Surveys," Metropolitan Atlanta Rapid Transit Authority, Planning and Policy Development, (April 1995).

(8) "82 Westheimer Low-Floor Bus Surveys," Metropolitan Transit Authority of Harris County (Internal Memo), (July 1997).

(9) "Customer and Bus Operator Research with the Low-Floor Bus," MTA New York City Transit, Marketing Research and Analysis, (January 1997).

(10) "Hybrid Electric/Low-Floor Bus Research," MTA New York City Transit, Marketing Research and Analysis, (March 1997).

(11) "Customer and Bus Operator Surveys on In-Service Test of New Flyer Low-Floor Bus," MTA New York City Transit Marketing Research and Analysis, (July 1997).

(12) "The Role of Passenger Amenities and Vehicle Characteristics in Building Transit Ridership," TCRP Project B-10, Interim Report, Project for Public Spaces, Inc., (March 1997).

(13) "An Evaluation of Accessible Transit Buses in Vancouver and Victoria," Final Report TP12709E, Transport Canada, (June 1995).

(14) "CTA Service Standards," Service Planning Section, (September 1990).

(15) "COST 322, Low-Floor Buses," Final Report EUR16707EN, European Commission, Directorate-General for Transport, (1995).

(16) "Altoona Bus Testing Reports," the Pennsylvania Transportation Institute, Report Numbers 9201, 9411-13, 9508-20, 9613-08-97, 9617-10-97, and 9708-15-97.

(17) "Kneeling buses take a pounding," News Article, The Globe and Mail, (October 15, 1997).

(18) "Standard Bus Procurement Guidelines, Part 5 - Technical Specifications Baseline Heavy-Duty Transit Bus" (draft), American Public Transit Association, (June 1997).

(19) "Accessible Ridership Report, Memorandum," New York City Transit, Department of Buses, (November 20, 1997).

(20) "Top Twenty Road Calls by Fleet and System-Wide MDBF Report," New York City Transit, Department of Buses, (November 1997).

(21) "Road Calls by Fleet and System-Wide MDBF Report - 1997," New York City Transit, Department of Buses, (January 1998).

(22) ANSI/ASHRAE Standard 62-1989, "Ventilation for Acceptable Indoor Air Quality," American Society of Heating, Refrigerating, and Air Conditioning Engineers, Inc., Atlanta, GA. (1990).

(23) ANSI/ASHRAE Standard 55-1992, "Thermal Environmental Conditions for Human Occupancy," American Society of Heating, Refrigerating, and Air Conditioning Engineers, Inc., Atlanta, GA. (1992).

(24) "Canadian Urban Transit Association Bus Ventilation Study, Phases 1, 2, 3, and 4," Envirotest, Inc. Reports 1, 2, 3, and 4, (November 1993 through June 1996).

(25) Transport Canada Transportation Department Center, "Nova Bus LFS Urban Bus Ventilation System Testing (Phase 5)," Environtest, Inc., Report 5, (May 1996).

(26) Levine, S.C. and G. Torng, "Dwell Time Effects on the Low-Floor Bus Design," Journal of Transportation Engineering, ASCE, Vol. 120, No. 6, (November/December 1994).

(27) Spiller, D. And L. Labell, "Operational Assessment of Paralympics Transit System: Low-Floor Buses, Lift-Equipped Buses, and Signage," Final Report, DOT-VNTSC-FTA-97-1, (February 1997).

(28) Cost Savings from Free Fare for People with Disabilities, AATA Memorandum, (February 1997).

(29) 1997 Transit Fact Book, American Public Transit Association.

(30) Summary of Canadian Transit Statistics, 1996 Data, Canadian Urban Transit Association.

(31) Rutenberg, U., "Urban Transit Bus Accessibility Concerns," Canadian Urban Transit Association, TCRP Report 10 (August 1995).

(32) Rutenberg, U., "Advanced Concepts to Accommodate Mobility Aids on Canadian Low-Floor Buses," Canadian Urban Transit Association, TCRP Report 15, (Forthcoming).

(33) Tests to Determine Regular Service and Emergency Acceleration Forces, Performed by GOTransit, (May 1993).

(34) Technical Developments and Configuration Decisions, Northrop Grumman, Bi-Monthly Report, (March/April, 1995).

(35) Advanced Technology Transit Bus, FY94 Technology Validation Final Report, Volume II Technical Report Updates, Northrop Grumman, (March 1995).

ACRONYMS AND ABBREVIATIONS

Bus Manufacturers

Gillig Corporation	GIL
Flxible Corporation	FLX
Motor Coach Industries International	MCI
Neoplan USA Corporation	NEO
New Flyer Industries Limited	NFIL
North American Bus Industries	NABI
Nova Bus Corporation	NOV
Orion Bus Industries	OBI
Transportation Manufacturing Corporation	TMC

Transit Agencies

Ann Arbor Transportation Authority	AATA
BC Transit - Victoria Regional Transit System	VRTS
Calgary Transit	CT
Capital District Transportation Authority	CDTA
Champaign-Urbana Mass Transit District	MTD
Chicago Transit Authority	CTA
Metropolitan Atlanta Rapid Transit Authority	MARTA
Metropolitan Transit Authority of Harris County	MTA
MTA New York City Transit	NYCT
Milwaukee County Transit System	MCTS
Phoenix Transit System	PTS
Société Transport de la Communauté Urbaine de Montréal	STCUM
Société de Transport de la Rive-Sud de Montréal	STRSM

Government Agencies

Federal Transit Administration	FTA
Transportation Research Board	TRB
Volpe National Transportation Systems Center	VNTSC

Organizations

American Public Transit Association	APTA
Canadian Urban Transit Association	CUTA

APPENDIX A

TECHNICAL DESCRIPTION OF LOW-FLOOR FLEETS

TECHNICAL DESCRIPTION OF LOW-FLOOR FLEETS

A more complete description of the low-floor bus fleets that were included in the study is given in Table A-1.

Table A-1. Information on Low-Floor Fleets

Transit Agency	Fleet No.	Fleet Size (ft)	Seats	Fuel	Propulsion System Engine	Propulsion System Transmission	Tires	HVCA	Manufacturer and Model	
Ann Arbor Transportation Authority	22	40	36	D	DDC - 6V92	ZF HP500	(M) 275/70R	Roof Sutrac AC-3 Aux. Fl. Ht.	New Flyer Industries	D40LF
	15	35	28	D	DDC - 6V92	AL B400R				D35LF
BC Transit - Victoria Regional Transit System	36	40	36	D	DDC - 6V92	VOITH D 863	(B) 275/70R	Roof Sutrac (H/V) Aux. Fl. Ht.	New Flyer Industries	D40LF
	44	40	38	D	DDC 50					
Calgary Transit	50	40	36	D	DDC - 6V92	ZF HP500	(G) 275/70R	Rear Thermo King Aux. Fl. Ht.	New Flyer Industries	D40LF
	84	40	39	D	DDC 50	AL B400R				
Champaign-Urbana Mass Transit District	41	40	36	D	DDC - 6V92	ZF HP49	(B) 275/70R	Roof Sutrac AC-3 Aux. Fl. Ht.	New Flyer Industries	D40LF
				D	DDC 50	ZF HP500				
Capital District Transportation Authority	21	40	32	D	DDC 50	AL B400R	(B) 305/70R	Roof Thermo King Aux. Fl. Ht.	Orion Bus Industries	ORION VI
Chicago Transit Authority	63	40	39	D	DDC 50	ZF HP590	(M) 275/70R	Roof Thermo King Aux. Fl. Ht.	New Flyer Industries	D40LF
	2	40	39	D	Cummins 8.3	ZF HP590	(B) 275/70R			H40LF
	1	40	39	H	FUEL CELL	- - -	(M) 275/70R			
Metropolitan Atlanta Rapid Transit Authority	118	40	40	CNG	DDC 50G	ZF HP500	(M) 275/70R	Rear Thermo King	New Flyer Industries	C40LF
	51	40	39	D	DDC 50	AL B400R				D40LF
Milwaukee County Transit System	146	40	39	D	DDC 50	AL B400R	(B) 305/70R	Rear Thermo King Aux. Fl. Ht.	New Flyer Industries	D40LF
Phoenix Transit System	93	40	37	D	DDC 50	AL B400R	(B) 275/70R	Rear Thermo King	New Flyer Industries	D40LF
Sault Ste. Marie Transit	4	40	36	D	DDC 50	AL B400R	(B) 305/70R		Orion Bus Industries	ORION VI
Société de Transport de la Communauté Urbaine de Montréal (STCUM)	270	40	39 (32)[a]	D	Cummins 8.3	AL B400R	(M) 305/70R	MCC Heating & Vent.	Nova Bus	LFS
Société de Transport de la Rive-Sud de Montréal (STRSM)	28	40	39 (38)[b]	D	Cummins 8.3	AL B400R	(M) 305/70R	MCC Heating & Vent.	Nova Bus	LFS

[a] STCUM has a test seating arrangement with less seats to facilitate passenger flow.
[b] STRSM replaced two forward facing seats behind the driver with an aisle facing seat.

APPENDIX B

DISCUSSIONS OF FACTORS IMPACTING CAPACITY

DISCUSSIONS OF FACTORS IMPACTING CAPACITY

The theoretical maximum number of passengers that can be carried on a line is a function of the capacity of the buses operating on the line and the average headway between buses on the line. The formula used to calculate the capacity of a line is: $C = B \times 60/H$.

Where:
    $C =$ capacity of the line, usually expressed as passengers per hour per direction (ppdph),
    $B =$ the capacity of the bus, expressed as the maximum number of passengers the bus can carry, and
    $H =$ the average operational headway of buses operating on the line, expressed in minutes.

The number of buses required for a line is a function of the length of the line, the average headway between buses, the average operating speed for the line, and the duration of layovers at the ends of the line. The number of buses required for a line can be estimated by the following formula: $TNB = (60 \times LL / S + 2 \times LT) / H$.

Where:
    $TNB =$ the total number of buses,
    $LL =$ the length of the line in miles,
    $S =$ the average speed along the line, in miles per hour,
    $LT =$ the layover time, in minutes, and
    $H =$ The average operating headway, in minutes.

The average speed, S, along a line is a function of the number of stops along the line, the average dwell time per stop, and the average time that is required to move from stop to stop. Line attributes such as whether or not it is an exclusive bus lane and does a bus have priority at intersections affect the average speed. The average dwell time is a function of the average boarding and alighting times for passengers, method of fare collection (can more than one door be used for boarding), and the average time required to re-enter the traffic stream if the bus is operating in a mixed traffic lane. The following formula (Reference B-1) can be used to approximate the average speed of a bus along a line:

$$S = \frac{D}{T + D/C + C(\tfrac{1}{2}a + \tfrac{1}{2}d)}$$

Where:
    $S =$ average bus speed,
    $T =$ average dwell time at stops,
    $D =$ average distance between stops
    $C =$ average cruising speed in lane (e.g., 50 kph),
    $a =$ average rate of acceleration of bus (e.g., 5 kph/sec.), and
    $d =$ average rate of deceleration of bus (e.g., 6 kph/sec.).

The average speeds of the transit agencies interviewed ranged from 25 to 16 kph (15.5 to 9.9 mph). The minimum headway was reported to be two minutes.

(B-1) Quinby, H.D., "Mass Transportation Characteristics," in Transportation and Traffic Engineering Handbook, Institute of Transportation Engineers, Prentice Hall, New Jersey (1976).

APPENDIX C

INTERVIEW GUIDE AND SURVEY FORM

INTERVIEW GUIDE AND SURVEY FORM

The interview guide that was used for the site visits to the transit agencies and the survey form that was given to all six of the heavy-duty bus manufacturers that are offering low-floor buses to agencies are provided in the following pages.

INTERVIEW GUIDE for TCRP PROJECT ON
"NEW DESIGNS AND OPERATING EXPERIENCES WITH LOW-FLOOR BUSES

PURPOSE: TO GATHER AND SYNTHESIZE INFORMATION AVAILABLE AS TO THE OPERATING EXPERIENCES OF TRANSIT AGENCIES THAT CURRENTLY OPERATE LOW-FLOOR BUSES, INCLUDING USER SATISFACTION AND ACCEPTANCE, SAFETY, NOTABLE FEATURES AND CONCERNS, AND IMPACTS ON RIDERSHIP, MAINTENANCE, AND OPERATIONS.

AGENCY NAME _____   DATE _____

CONTACT _____   TEL _____

TITLE _____   FAX _____

ADDRESS _____
(STREET)

_____
(CITY)   (STATE)   (ZIP)

FLEET INFORMATION

- TOTAL FLEET SIZE: _____   PEAK: AM ____ PM ____ BASE: ____

- LOW-FLOOR FLEET

SIZE	NO.	MANUFACTURER	DELIVERY DATE
40-FOOT			
35-FOOT			
60-FOOT			
≤30-FOOT			

- REASONS FOR PURCHASING LOW-FLOOR BUSES: _____
_____

- PLANNED FLEET IN 5 YEARS: _____ % LOW-FLOOR

- CAN YOU PROVIDE A COPY OF THE SEATING ARRANGEMENT?

CUSTOMER SATISFACTION/ACCEPTANCE

- DO YOU HAVE ANY SURVEYS/REPORTS ON CUSTOMER SATISFACTION AND ACCEPTANCE OF LOW-FLOOR BUSES? IF YES, CAN COPIES BE PROVIDED?

  DID THESE STUDIES INCLUDE BOTH AMBULATORY, DISABLED, AND SENIOR PASSENGERS, AND DID THE ANALYSIS EXAMINE THE RESPONSES FROM EACH GROUP SEPARATELY?

  DO YOU HAVE OTHER SOURCES OF INFORMATION ON CUSTOMER SATISFACTION OR ACCEPTANCE OF LOW-FLOOR BUSES, SUCH AS: PASSENGER COMPLAINT DATA OR OPERATOR REPORTS?

  TYPES OF CUSTOMER SATISFACTION/ACCEPTANCE INFORMATION SOUGHT INCLUDED:

  - BOARDING/ALIGHTING -- EASE, ENTRANCE/EXIT HEIGHTS, RAMPS
  - PASSENGER COMFORT -- HEATING/VENTILATION, A/C, NOISE, VIBRATION
  - PASSENGER VIEW -- HEIGHT, WINDOWS FOGGING UP, ROAD SPRAY
  - SEATING -- LACK, ARRANGEMENT, PERCEPTION OF INTERIOR SPACE
  - HAND HOLDS/PASSENGER ASSISTS -- LOCATION AND ADEQUACY
  - SAFETY & SECURITY -- INCLUDING PERCEPTIONS
  - FLOOR -- BI LEVEL (INTERIOR STEPS), SLOPES (OVER AXLE)
  - EXIT DOOR BEHIND REAR AXLE
  - LOCATION OF RAMP -- FRONT DOOR VERSUS REAR DOOR
  - OTHER

- HAVE THE LOW-FLOOR BUSES ATTRACTED DIFFERENT CUSTOMERS (e.g. MORE OLDER AND LESS MOBILE PEOPLE)?

OPERATIONAL EXPERIENCES

- WHAT HAVE BEEN YOUR EXPERIENCES WITH OPERATING YOUR LOW-FLOOR BUSES? TYPES OF INFORMATION DESIRED INCLUDE THE FOLLOWING:

    - IMPACTS ON RIDERSHIP

    - CAPACITY ISSUES WITH FEWER SEATS (WAS ADDITIONAL SERVICE ADDED TO COMPENSATE)?

    - DWELL TIME AND SCHEDULE IMPACTS

    - BOARDING/ALIGHTING TIMES - - AMBULATORY, SENIORS, DISABLED

    - MOBILITY DEVICE LOCATION

    - FARE COLLECTION ERGONOMICS

    - EXIT DOOR BEHIND REAR AXLE

    - RIDE QUALITY

    - FLOW OF PASSENGERS (ESPECIALLY BETWEEN FRONT WHEEL HOUSINGS)

    - UNCONVENTIONAL SEATING (e.g. REARWARD FACING, SEATS ON PEDESTALS)

    - OTHER

DO YOU HAVE AVAILABLE REPORTS/DATA ON ANY OF THE ABOVE TOPICS? CAN YOU PROVIDE COPIES?

OPERATIONAL EXPERIENCES (continued)

- HAVE YOU HAD ANY PROBLEMS WITH ANY OF THE FOLLOWING?

    - ROAD CLEARANCES OF THE BUS (damage due to lack of clearances)

    - DRIVING/HANDLING (road conditions: dry, snow, ice, wet)

    - DRIVING IN HIGH WATER

    - WATER OR DUST INTRUSION INSIDE THE BUS

    - WINTER OPERATIONS (e.g. windows fogging up, passenger comfort)

    - DRAINAGE OR BUILD UP OF SNOW OR ICE IN DOOR AREAS

    - PASSENGER VISIBILITY (road spray on windows)

    - OPERATOR VISIBILITY (e.g. road spray on windows/mirrors, glare)

    - NOISE (interior and/or exterior) OR VIBRATION

    - RAMP BOARDING FROM STREET LEVEL (i.e. no curb)

    - RAMP OPERATIONS, FRONT/REAR

    - KNEELING

    - OPERATING RANGE

    - BRAKING

    - TRACTION

    - OPERATION OF ROOF HATCHES (e.g. too high to open/close)

    - EMERGENCY EXIST

ARE REPORTS OR DATA AVAILABLE ON ANY OF THE ABOVE TOPICS?

MAINTENANCE EXPERIENCES

WHAT HAS BEEN YOUR EXPERIENCES WITH THE MAINTENANCE OF THE LOW-FLOOR BUSES? CAN YOU PROVIDE INFORMATION ON ANY OF THE FOLLOWING (including comparison with high-floor bus maintenance experience)?

- MAINTENANCE COSTS
- ROADCALLS (i.e. frequency)
- SERVICING THE LOW-FLOOR BUSES ON THE STREET (i.e. special tools)
- RAMP MAINTENANCE (including comparison with lift maintenance)
- TIRE WEAR OR EXCESSIVE DAMAGE
- SPECIAL TOOLS AND EQUIPMENT
- FACILITIES MODIFICATIONS (i.e. changes to hoists or pits)
- ACCESSIBILITY (i.e. systems and equipment mounted in roof area)
- INDEPENDENT FRONT SUSPENSION OR FRONT AXLES
- BRAKE WEAR
- FLOOR CLEANING

SAFETY EXPERIENCES

WHAT HAS BEEN YOUR EXPERIENCES WITH RESPECT TO SAFETY WITH YOUR LOW-FLOOR BUSES? CAN YOU PROVIDE INFORMATION ON ANY OF THE FOLLOWING?

- SLIPS AND FALLS WHILE BOARDING AND ALIGHTING
- SLIPS AND FALLS ON-BOARD
- INTERIOR STEP INCIDENTS
- RAMP INCIDENTS
- DOOR AND DOOR AREA INCIDENTS
- OTHER

OPERATOR SATISFACTION/ACCEPTANCE EXPERIENCES

WHAT HAS BEEN THE ACCEPTANCE OF YOUR LOW-FLOOR BUSES BY YOUR OPERATORS? HAVE YOU CONDUCTED ANY SURVEYS OF YOUR DRIVERS WITH RESPECT TO THE LOW-FLOOR BUSES?

DO YOU HAVE INFORMATION ON OPERATOR ACCEPTANCE OF ANY OF THE FOLLOWING?

- DRIVEABILITY AND HANDLING
- OPERATOR PLATFORM HEIGHT
- OPERATOR COMFORT - HEATING AND VENTILATION AND A/C
- ADEQUACY OF DEFROSTER SYSTEM
- VISION -- MIRRORS, GLARE, BLIND SPOTS
- SEPARATION OF PASSENGER AREA FROM OPERATOR'S COMPARTMENT
- FARE BOX ACCESSIBILITY
- PASSENGER FLOW

OTHER COMMENTS

_____

_____

_____

_____

_____

_____

_____

BUS MANUFACTURERS' SURVEY
FOR TCRP PROJECT ON

NEW DESIGNS AND OPERATING EXPERIENCES WITH LOW-FLOOR BUSES

PURPOSE: TO GATHER INFORMATION ON HEAVY-DUTY, LOW-FLOOR BUS TECHNOLOGY AND THE MARKET STATUS OF LOW-FLOOR BUSES AVAILABLE TO TRANSIT SYSTEMS IN THE U.S. AND CANADA.

NAME _____ DATE _____

CONTACT _____ TEL _____

TITLE _____ FAX _____

ADDRESS _____
(STREET)

_____
(CITY)   (STATE)   (ZIP)

STATUS OF LOW-FLOOR TECHNOLOGY

1) WHICH MODELS OF HEAVY-DUTY, LOW-FLOOR BUSES DO YOU OFFER OR PLAN TO OFFER TO THE TRANSIT MARKET? *(PLEASE CHECK ALL THAT APPLY)*

40-FOOT [ ]   35-FOOT [ ]   30-FOOT [ ]   ARTICS (55/60') [ ]

2) AT WHAT STAGES OF DEVELOPMENT ARE YOUR LOW-FLOOR BUS MODELS? *(PLEASE CHECK THE STAGE OF DEVELOPMENT FOR EACH MODEL)*

	40-FT	35-FT	30-FT	ARTICS
DESIGN				
PROTOTYPE				
PRODUCTION				

STATUS OF LOW-FLOOR TECHNOLOGY (continued)

3) WHICH TYPES OF PROPULSION SYSTEMS ARE AVAILABLE (OR ARE PLANNED TO BE AVAILABLE) FOR YOUR LOW-FLOOR BUSES? *(PLEASE CHECK ALL THAT APPLY)*

MODEL	40-FT		35-FT		30-FT		ARTICS	
PROPULSION OPTIONS	AV	PL	AV	PL	AV	PL	AV	PL
IC with MECHANICAL POWERTRAIN DIESEL								
CNG								
LNG								
LPG								
METHANOL/ETHANOL								
HYBRID-ELECTRIC POWERTRAIN DIESEL IC with TM [a]								
IC with TM [b]								
DIESEL IC with WHM [c]								
IC with WHM [d]								
ELECTRIC POWERTRAIN TROLLEY								
BATTERY								
FUEL CELL								

[a] Diesel engine with an electric traction motor.
[b] Other than diesel engine with an electric traction motor.
[c] Diesel engine with wheel hub motors.
[d] Other than diesel engine with wheel hub motors.

4) PLEASE PROVIDE INFORMATION ON THE TECHNICAL SPECIFICATIONS AND OPTIONS OF YOUR LOW-FLOOR BUSES ON THE FORMS PROVIDED, PAGES 4 AND 5, OR PROVIDE BROCHURES WITH THE INFORMATION.

5) PLEASE PROVIDE A DRAWING(s) OF YOUR MAXIMUM SEATING ARRANGEMENT.

6) PLEASE PROVIDE INFORMATION ON THE TYPE OF ELECTRICAL SYSTEM MULTIPLEX THAT IS USED.

MARKETING STATUS OF LOW-FLOOR BUSES

1) PLEASE PROVIDE THE NUMBER OF HEAVY-DUTY, LOW-FLOOR BUSES (12 YEAR) DELIVERED BY MODEL AND BY YEAR IN THE FOLLOWING TABLE.

YEAR	40-FT	35-FT	30-FT	ARTICS
1991				
1992				
1993				
1994				
1995				
1996				
1997				

2) PLEASE PROVIDE THE NUMBER OF HEAVY-DUTY, LOW-FLOOR BUSES YOU HAVE ON ORDER BY MODEL.

	40-FT	35-FT	30-FT	ARTICS
ON ORDER				

3) WHAT PERCENTAGE OF YOUR TOTAL BUS SALES IN 1996 WAS FOR LOW-FLOOR BUS MODELS? _____ WHAT PERCENTAGE DO YOU ANTICIPATE IT WILL BE IN 2000? _____

4) IS THERE A COST DIFFERENTIAL FOR LOW-FLOOR BUSES OVER COMPARABLE HIGH-FLOOR MODELS? YES [ ] NO [ ]

   IF YES, WHAT IS THE TYPICAL DIFFERENTIAL? _____

TECHNICAL SPECIFICATIONS OF LOW-FLOOR BUSES

CHARACTERISTICS	40-FT	35-FT	30-FT	ARCTIC
MODEL IDENTIFICATION				
WIDTH, inches				
HEIGHT, inches				
WHEELBASE, inches				
TURNING RADIUS, feet				
MEASURED APPROACH ANGLE, degrees				
MEASURED DEPARTURE ANGLE, degrees				
MEASURED BREAKOVER ANGLE, degrees				
MEASURED CLEARANCE IN AXLE AREA, in.				
1st DOOR ENT. HT. (not kneeled), inches				
2nd DOOR EXIT HT. (not kneeled), inches				
KNEELING CAPABILITY: FRONT DOOR (in inches) REAR DOOR				
TYPE OF KNEELING: FRONT, SIDE, BOTH				
FRONT DOOR WIDTH, inches				
REAR DOOR WIDTH, inches				
RAMP LOCATION, FRONT/REAR DOOR				
WHEELCHAIR LOCATION, FRONT/REAR				
NUMBER OF SEATS [a]				
NUMBER OF STANDEES [b]				
GVWR, POUNDS				
CURB WEIGHT, POUNDS				

[a] Maximum number of seats with two wheelchair positions (no wheelchair riders on board) using a hip to knee room of approximately 26.5 inches.

[b] Use 1.5 square feet of free floor space per standee.

OPTIONS OFFERED ON LOW-FLOOR BUSES
(PLEASE ADD OTHER OPTIONS OFFERED)

OPTION	YES	NO	ADDITIONAL INFORMATION
AIR CONDITIONING			
ROOF			
REAR OF BUS			
OPENABLE WINDOWS			TYPES?
REAR WINDOW			
FORCED AIR HEATING FOR THE FLOOR AREA			
WARM WALL HEATING			
2ND DOOR LOCATION:			
IN FRONT OF REAR AXLE			
BEHIND REAR AXLE			
NUMBER OF DOORS			2 [ ] 3 [ ]
DOOR WIDTHS			
BUS WIDTH, 96" / 102"			ONLY 102" [ ] ONLY 96" [ ]
ELECTRIC PROPULSION			
ALTERNATIVE FUELED PROPULSION			
PROVIDE LIST OF ENGINE OPTIONS			
PROVIDE LIST OF TRANSMISSION OPTIONS			
PROVIDE LIST OF TIRE OPTIONS			
ELECTRICAL SYSTEM MULTIPLEX OPTIONS			

APPENDIX D

LISTING OF PARTICIPANTS

LISTING OF PARTICIPANTS

The following transit agencies and bus manufacturers participated in this study.

Transit Agencies

Ann Arbor Transportation Authority
BC Transit - Victoria Regional Transit System
Calgary Transit
Champaign-Urbana Mass Transit District
Capital District Transportation Authority
Chicago Transit Authority
Metropolitan Atlanta Rapid Transit Authority
Metropolitan Transit Authority of Harris County
Milwaukee County Transit System
Phoenix Transit System
Sault Ste. Marie Transit
Société de Transport de la Communauté Urbaine de Montréal
Société de Transport de la Rive-Sud de Montréal

Bus Manufacturers

Gillig Corporation
Neoplan USA Corporation
New Flyer Industries Limited
North American Bus Industries
Nova Bus Corporation
Orion Bus Industries